Caldecott Connections to Language Arts

Caldecott Connections to Language Arts

Shan Glandon

2000
LIBRARIES UNLIMITED, INC.
Englewood, Colorado

To writers and artists and all those who celebrate imagination.

Libraries Unlimited, Inc.
P.O. Box 6633
Englewood, CO 80155-6633
1-800-237-6124
www.lu.com

Library of Congress Cataloging-in-Publication Data

Glandon, Shan.
  Caldecott connections to language arts / Shan Glandon.
      p. cm.
  Includes bibliographical references and index.
  ISBN 1-56308-846-0 (pbk.)
    1. Language arts (Elementary)--United States--Curricula. 2. Caldecott Medal. 3. Illustrated children's books--Study and teaching--United States. 4. Education, Elementary--Activity programs--United States. I. Title.

  LB1576 .G474 2000
  372.6'043--dc21   00-041218
P

Contents

Figures and Activity Sheets

Figures

Activity Sheets

Introduction

➤ Connecting to the Curriculum

Caldecott Award literature provides fuel for teaching, extending, and enriching curriculum objectives. The award winners are engaging stories that offer vivid vocabulary images, use art in varied ways, and spark links to each of the major curriculum areas.

Students may begin the year with a look at Randolph Caldecott and the award itself (see the lesson introducing Randolph Caldecott and reading the honor books on page 225), and Caldecott Award posters may be displayed in the classroom and the library as constant reminders of all the stories that have won. (Caldecott Award posters are available from Perma-Bound, 617 East Vandalia Rd., Jacksonville, IL 62650, 800-637-6581; cost: $2.00.) The Caldecott Medal, named in honor of Randolph Caldecott, a nineteenth-century children's illustrator, has been awarded annually since 1938 to an American illustrator for the most distinguished picture book published during the previous year. When reviewing books for the award, committee members look for excellence in artistic technique as well as in integrating the text of the story into the pictorial interpretation. Randolph Caldecott was chosen because he established new directions in illustrating children's books. His illustrations were drawn with the child in mind; they have humor and imagination and are filled with lifelike characters, lots of action, and many details. The Caldecott Web site (http://www.ala.org/alsc/caldecott.html) can be bookmarked and students can browse for further information and enjoyment.

➤ Connecting to Art

Connections with art teachers are a natural result of a focus on Caldecott Award literature and offer opportunities for students to try different illustrating techniques as they explore line, color, tone, and balance in art. Students can easily re-create imaginative scenes from *The Polar Express* using blue construction paper (simulates pastel paper because of its texture) and oil pastels. They can make wonderful animal masks to dramatize *Fables* by using large brown paper bags, pencils for outlining and details, and gouache paints for filling in lines with bright colors. Investigating the effects of string lines (straight, curvy, thick and thin, and slanted) assists students in exploring techniques used in the illustrations of *Sam, Bangs, and Moonshine*. Watercolor paintings (like those in *The Fool of the World and the Flying Ship*, *Mirette on the High Wire*, and *Owl Moon*) provide students with opportunities to play with color to express mood and feelings in art. Hand-tinted woodcut illustrations (*Snowflake Bentley*) can be created using foam trays, scratching tools, and watercolor paints.

Another method for helping students experience the variety of media used in illustrating Caldecott Award literature is to gather samples of the different media. Take a trip to an art supply store and purchase the following supplies: paint samples (oil, acrylic, watercolor, gouache, gesso, and tempera), paintbrushes, a pen with several nibs, inks (India and one other), pastels (oil, Conté, and one other), pencils (grease, graphite, and colored), a small block of soft wood like pine or balsa (for woodcuts), and an Exacto knife (for the woodcuts). As the stories are shared and the art techniques are discussed, show the appropriate media and demonstrate their uses.

➤ Connecting to Curriculum Units

Caldecott Award stories can become the springboard for introducing units of studies. Language arts extensions build wonderful opportunities for developing the reader and the writer in each student. Traditional literature is introduced and studied through the fables and fairy tale units (*Fables, Rapunzel, Lon PoPo*, and *The Fool of the World and the Flying Ship*); creative writing and a focus on the strategies of the writing process come through *Mirette on the High Wire* (character sketching), *Owl Moon* (observation and descriptive writing), *The Polar Express* (recalling and writing memory stories), *Tuesday* (mysteries and a mystery magazine), *Sam, Bangs, and Moonshine* (acrostic and wish poetry), and *Time of Wonder* (seasonal poetry). The work described in the story *Snowflake Bentley* is a natural introduction to writing reports.

➤ Collaboration

Collaborations between classroom teachers and library media specialists facilitate implementation of the activities described in this book. The stories can be shared in the classroom or the library, and both the teacher and the librarian can assign, develop, and assess activities. The fairy tale unit (using *Rapunzel, Lon PoPo*, and *The Fool of the World and the Flying Ship*) requires this close connection because students choose fairy tales for independent reading, develop creative products that demand rehearsal space and time, research new settings for *The Fool of the World* alternatives, and culminate the unit with a tea party and display of their work. In the mystery unit that follows *Tuesday*, the library media specialist and the teacher can divide mentoring responsibilities and help students effectively work in their editorial roles; students also use the library to select mysteries for independent reading. Research is also a significant component of this unit as students find out about mysterious topics in history. Multiple resources can be provided by the library media specialist for the bird unit that develops from sharing *Owl Moon*. The library media specialist can give book talks to help students select character study novels and fairy tales for independent reading.

When implementing the *Time of Wonder* lesson plans, the following pattern of collaboration between the classroom and the library occurred. The story was introduced by the librarian; at the "Connect" stage of the lesson plan the teacher explained the art activity, and then the students returned to the classroom. The summer poem lessons were taught in the classroom; for the fall poem lessons students returned to the library, and the librarian taught these lessons in cooperation with the teacher. Haiku poems (winter) were a collaboration among the librarian, the classroom teacher, and the art teacher, who helped students complete the watercolor paintings for their poems. Spring poem lessons were taught in the classroom.

The lessons resulting from sharing *Owl Moon* followed this pattern of collaboration: The story was introduced in the library, and in the classroom the teacher helped students draw and paint favorite scenes from the book. The descriptive writing lessons were led by the teacher in the classroom, whereas the introductory lesson on birds was led by the librarian in the media center, and the librarian accompanied the teacher and the students on their bird-watching expedition. The web that resulted from this lesson also remained on a library bulletin board during the rest of the unit. While the teacher led the feathers lesson and the construction of the bird feeders, the librarian facilitated small research groups working on bird habitats. This allowed more individualized time in the classroom. The food chain, owl pellets, and nest lessons were also completed in the classroom; then students were ready for fact/fable research, which was led by the librarian. During fact/fable research the students and the teacher came to the library each day for a block of research time (forty-five minutes to an hour). The final lesson plans were completed in the classroom.

➤ Integrating Multiple Intelligences Theory and Practices

In *Frames of Mind: The Theory of Multiple Intelligences* (New York: Basic Books, 1983), Howard Gardner challenges the narrowly held definition of intelligence (based on an IQ score) and the context in which IQ had been measured (completing isolated tasks outside of a natural learning environment) and proposes a theory of multiple intelligences that identifies at least eight basic intelligences and defines intelligence as the capacity for solving problems and fashioning products in a context-rich and naturalistic setting. *Verbal/linguistic intelligence* is the capacity to use words effectively, either in writing (exemplified by poets, authors, playwrights, journalists, and editors) or in speaking (storytelling and debating). Students who exhibit this intelligence pore over words, are fascinated with language, and use language effectively in speaking and/or writing. Those with *musical/rhythmic intelligence* respond to sounds and rhythms and enjoy and seek out opportunities to hear music, to improvise and play with sounds and rhythms, and to seek musical mentors. Notice these students: They often tap their feet or pencils, sometimes hum while working intently, and perk up when music or rhythm is used during a lesson. *Visual/spatial intelligence* is defined by an ability to see the visual-spatial world accurately and express those images through painting, drawing, designing, and sculpting. Because they see internally, students with highly developed visual/spatial intelligence are also often good at chess and navigation (finding their way in uncharted spaces); they may also be daydreamers. These are the artists who love anything visual, who see images and pictures and draw their ideas. *Bodily/kinesthetic intelligence* is found in dancers, athletes, and inventors because of their prowess in using body movement to express ideas and feelings and to implement games or to use their hands to create new products or transform things. Think of students who learn best by doing; if they can manipulate it, do it, create movements to learn it, then they develop understanding. *Logical/mathematical intelligence* involves skill with numbers and number manipulation and in strategies for reasoning—scientific, deductive, and inductive. Problem solving interests these students, and they love the challenge of organizing and using numbers and developing charts, timelines, and graphs as expressions of thinking. Students with highly developed *interpersonal intelligence* easily communicate and work collaboratively with others; they are sensitive to feelings and moods. These students are good listeners who work well in collaborative situations and seem to get along with anyone. They have a knack for bringing out the best in each learner. *Intrapersonal intelligence* focuses on self-knowledge and the ability to act on the basis of that knowledge. These students are reflective, thoughtful learners who need to see the big picture and have time to fit new knowledge into current thinking; they enjoy building awareness of their own processes for learning. The eighth intelligence, *naturalist intelligence*, focuses on a student's ability to observe and make connections in living things (plants and animals) and in natural phenomena (clouds, rocks). This intelligence highlights the accomplishments of scientists in creating classification systems.

Gardner suggests that everyone possesses all eight intelligences, but some are highly developed, others more modestly developed, and still others are relatively undeveloped, and that most people can develop each intelligence to an adequate level of competency. This understanding has implications for the organization and development of daily lesson plans because integration of multiple intelligences theory and practice expands opportunities for students to mobilize their full range of intellectual abilities and become thoroughly engaged in learning.

➤ Designing the Lessons

Best-practice principles emerging from state-of-the-art teaching in each curriculum field focus on learning that is student centered (builds on students' natural curiosity), experiential (hands-on and active), holistic (involves big-picture ideas), authentic (involves encounters with complex and real ideas), expressive (demands the whole range of intelligence, including art, music, writing, speaking, etc.), reflective (allows time to generalize and make connections), social (includes support of peers and mentors), collaborative (encourages working together rather than in competition), democratic (models the principles of living and working in a democracy), cognitive (demands higher-order thinking), developmental (involves learning experiences guided by the needs of the students), constructivist (builds, creates, develops knowledge systems), and challenging (provides choices and responsibility for learning). Two books to read for more information about these principles are *Best Practice* by Steven Zemelman, Harvey Daniels, and Arthur Hyde (Heinemann, 1998) and *ITI: The Model, Integrated Thematic Instruction* by Susan Kovalik (Books for Educators, 1994). They can be ordered from Heinemann, 361 Hanover St., Portsmouth, NH 03801-3912; cost: $23.50 and from Books for Educators, 17051 S.E. 272nd St., Suite 18, Kent, WA 98042; cost: $27.50.

The "Engage, Elaborate, Explore, Connect" lesson plan format that I developed in 1994 is the organizing structure for the story units. This lesson planning format integrates best-practice principles, builds a discovery approach to learning, promotes integration of multiple intelligences theory and practice, and lets teachers see, at a glance, diversity and flexibility in teaching.

Engage

Teachers use this one-to-three-minute step to engage the attention of the student; it's a wake-up call to the brain and a way to start the brain thinking about patterns and relationships. Through a puzzling picture, a catchy musical piece, a challenging question, complicated body movements, a paradox, or a series of quick visual images, the "Engage" step provides the spark that captures the total interest of the students and prepares them for the lesson content. Some of the "Engage" sections include "quick think" activities. The goal of a quick think is to awaken the brain and have students begin to think in open-ended ways.

Elaborate

In this portion of the lesson, teachers use multiple intelligence strategies to elaborate important concepts and skills. Teachers may use stories, video footage, creative dramatics, debate, dance and movement, questioning, and rhythms to teach lesson content.

Explore

This step gives the students opportunities to explore lesson content and develop in-depth investigations and studies.

Connect

This is the step in which students make connections to real-world settings through reflection, generalization, synthesis, and transformation, thus enhancing the capacity for solving problems and fashioning products.

When using this organizing format, there are many starting points. Sometimes the "Explore" activity is clear in my mind and I work from that activity. I then decide what direct instruction is needed for successful completion of the activity. (This direct instruction becomes the "Elaborate" stage of the lesson.) With these two components developed, I think about capturing students' attention, awakening the brain for learning, and sparking an interest. The "Engage" step of the lesson helps students "tune in" and get ready for the complexity of thought and work required for the rest of the lesson. Music, art, and movement are particularly effective attention-getters in the "Engage" step, and I enjoy challenging myself to use them. Then, based on these three components of the lesson, I think about making connections and demonstrating understandings and ask myself: "How will students reflect on the activity and demonstrate and share what they have learned?"

Because language arts lessons focus so intensely on words, I really look to art, music, dance and movement, and observation of the natural world as key ingredients for designing the lessons. If our "Explore" activity is writing, then our "Engage" and "Elaborate" activities need to be experiences that build powerful imagery and expression. I think of a third-grade teacher who developed a file of pictures, music, and observation opportunities, which, as she said, "allowed students to see with the eye of a writer, e.g., Robert Frost, and see what prompted him to write 'Stopping by the Woods on a Snowy Night.' "

Caldecott Connections brings award-winning literature to the language arts curriculum. I hope you enjoy the fun and diversity offered in the activities and the noise and excitement produced when students are actively engaged in constructing knowledge. I also hope these activities inspire continuing connections for you and your students.

1 Fables

Written by Arnold Lobel
Illustrated by Arnold Lobel
New York: Harper & Row, 1980

Summary

➤ In this collection of twenty fables, an array of animal characters from a crocodile to an ostrich share lessons in love, humility, being true to oneself, giving and receiving advice, wishing, and flattery.

Award Year

➤ 1981

Art Information

➤ Illustrated using gouache and pencil.

Curriculum Connections

➤ Folklore: animal stories, with an emphasis on fables

➤ Activity Plan 1: Sharing the Story

Materials

Zomo the Rabbit: A Trickster Tale from West Africa told and illustrated by Gerald
    McDermott (New York: Harcourt Brace Jovanovich, 1992)
Why Mosquitoes Buzz in People's Ear by Verna Aardema, pictures by Leo Dillon and
    Diane Dillon (New York: Dial Press, 1975)
Caldecott Award poster
Sketching pencil (available at art supply stores)
Tube of gouache pigment (available at art supply stores)

Engage

Because animals are the main characters of fables and are used to illustrate human behaviors, animal riddles are a fun way to introduce fables and get students looking at the distinctive behaviors and characteristics of animals. Read each clue slowly and pause frequently to let students think and begin to guess the animals that are described (*Verbal/Linguistic Intelligence*):

I am very intelligent and, contrary to what people say, I like to keep clean. I roll in
    the mud and dust to keep insects off my nice pink skin. My nose is strong and
    flat, very good for pressing to the ground as I root around for the plants and bulbs
    I like to eat. What am I? (pig)

I live on my own, slinking quietly along the ground as I hunt through the night. I
    carry my kill up into a tree where I can eat it and stay safe from lions and jackals.
    I am very strong; I can drag prey of my own weight up into a tree if I need to. I
    live in Africa and South Asia and my call is a hollow, coughing roar. What am I?
    (panther)

I am very small. I have tiny hands to hold things. People aren't happy to have me in
    their houses because I nibble on lots of things. I like to find a warm nook or
    cranny in a tree or underneath a shed where I can hibernate. If I am disturbed, I
    squeak. What am I? (mouse)

I am very small—only about as big as a hamster. I am the only mammal that can fly.
    I live in caves and abandoned houses because I like the dark. People say that I'm
    not very pretty, but I am very well groomed; I clean myself like a cat. I eat insects
    and have a high, squeaky voice. What am I? (bat)

The feathers on top of my head look like ears, but they're only for decoration. My real
    ears are tucked under the feathers by my eyes. My eyesight is very sharp, especially
    in the dark. I can turn my head almost all the way around as I watch for the mice
    and small birds I like to eat. I sit very still on a branch, and then swoop down
    soundlessly to catch them. When I call out, I hoot. What am I? (owl)

Elaborate

There are different kinds of animal stories in the folklore category. Figure 1.1 compares the different tales: trickster, fable, and pourquoi. Explain the three types to the students as follows:

	Trickster Tale	Fable	Pourquoi Tale
Characters	The central character is a wise trickster in animal shape. Lively characterization Animals act like humans.	There are one or two main characters who are animals. Flat characterization Animals act like humans.	Characters are animals. Lively characterization Animals act like humans.
Purpose	Tells how trickster uses his cleverness and mental prowess to solve a seemingly insolvable problem.	Teaches a lesson.	Explains in humorous and entertaining ways how animals got certain characteristics.

➤ **Figure 1.1. Comparing Animal Folklore**

Trickster stories have a main character, usually an animal, who outwits or is outwitted by another character; the character is small and weak (in body strength), but strong in cleverness, cunning, and resourcefulness. *Zomo the Rabbit* is an example of this kind of story. In the story, Zomo, a not very big, not very strong, but oh so clever rabbit, asks Sky God for wisdom; before Sky God grants his wish, he demands three impossible things: scales from the big fish, milk from the wild cow, and a tooth from the leopard. Zomo uses his courage, good sense, and resourcefulness to trick each animal into releasing what he needs, thus receiving wisdom from Sky God.

Discuss with students how they would acquire the impossible things. Remind them that trickster tales never use weapons, but tasks are accomplished through the cunning and skill of the small character. Ask students how they would gather scales from a big fish, milk from a wild cow, and a tooth from a leopard.

Pourquoi animal tales usually have titles like "Why the _____ has
_____." These are similar to legends, but are exaggerated and humorous
because they are not believed, but are created for entertainment. *Why
Mosquitoes Buzz in People's Ear* is an example of a pourquoi story. The
story begins as mosquito annoys iguana and iguana reacts and places sticks
in his ears to shut out the whine of mosquito. It continues with this chain
of events: iguana ignores python, who scares rabbit by slithering into his
hole, which sends rabbit scurrying in fright across the forest, which alarms
monkey, who screeches and leaps from tree to tree, accidentally killing
owlet, which causes Mother Owl to grieve and not wake the sun. King
Lion calls a council meeting to discover why Mother Owl won't wake the
sun, and slowly the council traces the cause to mosquito who, because he
has a guilty conscience, whines continually in people's ears.

Ask students to describe other pourquoi or to tell "why" stories they know. Ask them how the explanations are humorous and entertaining.

A third kind of story is a fable. That will be our example for today. Fables
are short tales that use animals as the main characters, and the actions of
the animals reveal a lesson or moral. The animals also have the magic
power to speak as humans do.

Ask if students are familiar with the fable of the "The Tortoise and the Hare" by Aesop; invite them
to share what they know about the story and then discuss the moral or lesson that is learned from the
story. (In this fable the tortoise and the hare race. Although hare leaps ahead and seems destined to
win, tortoise, because of its slow, steady progress, actually beats the hare, thus leading to the moral:
Perseverance and determination bring success in spite of the odds.)

Explore

Share some of the fables from Arnold Lobel's book, such as "The Ducks and the Fox,"
on page 5 (The duck sisters change their route to the pond after barely escaping capture by the fox, finally
realizing that a change in routine can be a positive action.); "The Hen and the Apple Tree," on page
11 (A wolf disguises himself as an apple tree and tries to trick hen, but hen is not fooled and reminds
wolf that it is always difficult to pretend to be something one is not.); "The Baboon's Umbrella," on
page 12 (Baboon foolishly listens to advice from his friend gibbon and suffers the consequences, a
soaking in the rain.); "The Elephant and His Son," on page 32 (Elephant Son tries not to disturb
Papa when he is reading his newspaper, but eventually interrupts his reading when the ashes from Papa's
cigar catch his slipper on fire, leading to the moral that knowledge cannot always take the place of
simple observation.); and "The Mouse at the Seashore," on page 40 (Mouse encounters many difficulties before reaching his goal: time at the seashore contentedly watching the moon and stars appear
over the ocean.).

After sharing one of the fables and giving its lesson, see if students can identify the
moral/lesson of subsequent fables that are shared.

Connect

Have students think about other lessons that might be learned and make sure they are firm in their understanding of the purpose of a fable (short, simple tale that teaches a lesson).
Share the Caldecott Award information:

1. As students examine the cover of the book, ask them what special thing they notice. (gold medal) Ask them what the name of the medal is. (Caldecott Award Medal) Ask them why it has been placed on this book. (Expect some of the following answers: The illustrations are special, well done, particularly interesting, exciting, and/or unusual.)

2. Discuss the art techniques used in creating the pictures. Pencil was one medium. (Show the pencil and slowly browse the pages, asking students to note how pencil is used in several of the illustrations. For example, penciled lines give definition to the fence and the fur and feathers of the fox and the ducks in "The Ducks and the Fox," on page 4; penciled lines help emphasize and create the motion of the stormy waves in "The Lobster and the Crab," on page 8; and penciled lines and squiggles are very evident in the illustration accompanying "The Ostrich in Love," on page 20.)

   Ask students what medium was used to add color to the illustrations. Show the illustrations for "The Frogs at the Rainbow's End," on page 14, and "The Camel Dances," on page 22, and have students speculate about the medium. Then tell the students: Gouache added the color. Gouache is a paint pigment that has been mixed with white chalk and water (show the tube of pigment). When it is applied, it looks a lot like a watercolor painting, as you can see in the rainbow in the frogs fable and the background sun and sand in the camel fable. (Show several other illustrations to emphasize the watercolor look of gouache; e.g., the sunset sky in "The Mouse at the Seashore," on page 40, the pink wall of the restaurant in "The Hippopotamus at Dinner," on page 38, and the light and shadow of lion's robe in "King Lion and the Beetle," on page 7.)

3. Ask two student volunteers to search the poster for the year the story won. (Searching the poster helps students become familiar with the many different titles selected for the award.)

➤ Activity Plan 2: Dramatizing Fables

Materials

Umbrella

Engage

Twirl an umbrella in front of the students and review "The Baboon's Umbrella," on page 12. Ask students to describe what happened in this story. (Baboon met his friend Gibbon and discussed his umbrella problem; Gibbon advised him to cut holes in it, which he foolishly did; he was happy until it rained and he was soaked.)

Elaborate

Ask students what elements would be important to show the class if they were to dramatize this story. (the two characters, Gibbon and Baboon, their close friendship, the umbrella that cannot be furled) Ask them how they would pantomime this story. Invite a student to participate with you in creating the pantomime using the instructions below; announce the moral before you begin. (*Bodily/Kinesthetic and Verbal/Linguistic Intelligences*)

BABOON'S UMBRELLA

Moral: Advice from friends is like the weather;
some of it is good and some of it is very bad.

Teacher (in role of Baboon): Enter the performance space and mess with your umbrella, looking annoyed; add monkey behaviors to your pantomime. Continue to try to furl the umbrella as your friend Gibbon enters the performance space.

Student (in role of Gibbon): Look happy to see your friend Baboon, perform some action of greeting that combines monkey behavior and human behavior, then look puzzled.

Teacher (in role of Baboon): Pantomime an explanation of the problem of the umbrella.

Student (in role of Gibbon): Pantomime the scissors suggestion.

Teacher (in role of Baboon): Look excited and hurry away from the performance space.

Student (in role of Gibbon): Look satisfied and pleased; perform some monkey action as you leave the performance space.

Teacher (in role of Baboon): Walk in, looking pleased and proud, as though basking in the sun, then frown, look up, blink (as though raindrops are beginning to fall), and stand as though you are drenched. Turn to the audience and repeat the moral: "Advice from friends is like the weather; some of it is good and some of it is very bad."

Explore

Share the steps in planning the dramatization. After rereading the fable and thinking about the pantomime, the umbrella was chosen as the prop because that would help the audience understand the dramatization; the rest of the pantomime could be told through the facial and body expressions of the characters: the happiness at the meeting of good friends, the behavior of listening intently to the advice, the reaction of excitement by baboon and pleasure by gibbon (after the advice is given), and the realization that the advice is bad as baboon is soaked and drenched. The goal in dramatizing the fable is to convey as realistically as possible the human personality characteristic each character represents: the foolishness of the baboon, the slyness of a fox, the kingliness of a lion, the craftiness of a wolf, the resourcefulness of a chicken, the silliness of a duck, and the humility of a small beetle.

List the fables that will be pantomimed and have students select the stories they wish to pantomime. (Figure 1.2 suggests fables that would be easy to pantomime, identifies the number of characters required for each pantomime, and gives ideas for suggested props.) Encourage students to keep props to a minimum, select only those costumes that are needed to convey the characters' personalities, and focus on facial and body expressions as the means for carrying the fable. Provide rehearsal time and circulate among the groups as they plan and rehearse, modeling body and facial interpretations.

Connect

Have the students perform the pantomimes. Reinforce the connections between the events of the stories and the morals that follow by discussing this question: What happened in the pantomime that led to the moral? The dramatizations and the discussions will continue to build understanding that the events of the fable lead to the moral, which will help make writing original fables an easier task.

➤ Activity Plan 3: An Apple a Day— Investigating Wise Sayings

Materials

Two apples and a knife (If you have a large class you may need three apples; each student should receive a slice.)
Drawing paper (one sheet per student)
Illustrating materials (colored pencils)
Proverb dictionaries (one per student partnership)

Engage

Slice the apples in front of the students and distribute the slices. Ask students if they have ever heard this proverb or wise saying, "An apple a day keeps the doctor away." Ask them if they know what it means and why it became a wise saying. (The nutrients from apples keep you healthy; if you are healthy you usually don't visit the doctor very often.)

Fables	Characters	Suggested Props
The Ducks and the Fox	two ducks and a fox	large cloth bag
King Lion and the Beetle	a lion and a beetle	clothing for the lion: cape, crown, jewels
The Lobster and the Crab	a lobster and a crab	boat
The Hen and the Apple Tree	a hen and a wolf	apple tree sandwich board
The Frogs at the Rainbow's End	three frogs and a snake	rainbow
The Poor Old Dog	a poor old dog and a wealthy dog	golden ring, tattered coat (old dog), fancy coat (wealthy dog)
The Bad Kangaroo	a small kangaroo, a principal, and Mr. and Mrs. Kangaroo	a thumbtack, a spitball, a loud booming noise
The Pelican and the Crane	a pelican and a crane	a plate of cookies
The Mouse at the Seashore	a mouse, his parents, and a cat	a mural showing the seashore

▶ Figure 1.2. Fables to Pantomime

Elaborate

Ask students how they would illustrate this proverb. Refocus question: What picture would show the meaning of this wise saying? Have students quickly sketch some ideas and share their illustrations. (Some responses may be strong muscles, lots of energy for soccer and other sports, the apple with vitamins and minerals coming from the top, a person saying "no more colds," etc.) (*Visual/Spatial Intelligence*)

Explore

Have students work with partners, using proverb dictionaries to find wise sayings/proverbs for these character traits: courage, compassion, teamwork, responsibility, respect, perseverance, honesty, self-discipline. Have students create pictures that explain the proverbs. (*Visual/Spatial and Interpersonal Intelligences*)

Connect

Share the proverb pictures with the class. Discuss why these are wise sayings.

➤ Activity Plan 4: Reading Aesop's Fables

Materials

Fortunately written and illustrated by Remy Charlip (New York: Four Winds Press, 1964)
"The Dove and the Snake" from *Aesop's Fables*, illustrated by Heidi Holder (New York: Viking Press, 1981)
Aesop's fables (one per student partnership)
Tagboard (cut into 6-x-6-inch squares, enough for five squares per student partnership)
Clear tape (to attach the squares)
Activity sheet 1.1, Storyboard Planning (one per student partnership)

Engage

Share Charlip's book, *Fortunately*, and discuss its format: a statement of good fortune followed by a statement of misfortune until the story ends with good fortune. (*Verbal/Linguistic Intelligence*)

Text continues on page 12.

Fable:
What fortunate experiences happen in the fable?
What unfortunate experiences happen in the fable?
What is the moral of the fable? What lesson is learned? Be sure to use your own words to tell the lesson.

►Activity Sheet 1.1. Storyboard Planning: Fortunately/Unfortunately Book

Title Panel Design:	Fortunately Statement 1 Design:
Unfortunately Statement Design:	Fortunately Statement 2 Design:
Moral of the Fable Design:	

➤Activity Sheet 1.1. Storyboard Planning: Fortunately/Unfortunately Book (*cont.*)

Elaborate

Use this fortunately/unfortunately structure to model how students will report on the Aesop's fables they read independently. Share "The Dove and the Snake" Aesop fable. Ask students: What fortunate experiences are told in the fable? (The dove was not caught by the snake and the snake startled the hunter, so the dove escaped.) What was unfortunate in the fable? (Because the dove watched the snake, the dove did not notice the hunter stalking it with his net.) Use the students' ideas to develop two fortunately statements and one unfortunately statement, for example: "Fortunately, the dove was not caught by the snake"; "Unfortunately, the dove failed to notice a hunter creeping closer with a net"; "Fortunately, the snake startled the hunter and in the confusion the dove flew to safety." Once these statements are constructed, have the students use their own words to state the moral of the story. (Even our worst enemies can help us.) (*Verbal/Linguistic Intelligence*)

Show the students how these statements will be used to create the accordion pleat panel displays shown in figure 1.3. Panel one gives the title and author of the fable and lists the students' names, panel two shows the first fortunately statement and includes an illustration, panel three displays the unfortunately statement and an illustration, panel four includes the second fortunately statement and an illustration, and panel five shows the moral of the fable. When the panels are completed, hook them together with wide tape.

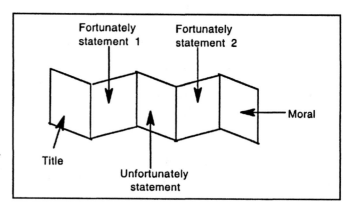

➤ Figure 1.3. Fortunately/Unfortunately Panel Display

Other fortunately/unfortunately examples you can use if students are stumped are:

"The Hare and the Tortoise": Fortunately, the tortoise had confidence in her speed. Unfortunately, the hare sprinted ahead and left the tortoise far behind. Fortunately, the hare stopped to nap and the tortoise reached the finish line first. Moral: Perseverance and determination help you succeed against great odds.

"The Fox and the Grapes": Fortunately, the fox found a vineyard full of ripe grapes. Unfortunately, they were out of his reach and he tried and tried but could not jump high enough to reach them. Fortunately, he convinced himself that they were sour. Moral: Sometimes we convince ourselves something we want is bad when we don't get it.

"The Horse and the Donkey": Fortunately, the donkey and the horse were traveling together. Unfortunately, the horse refused to carry any of the load and the donkey soon stumbled and fell. Fortunately, the donkey was relieved of his load and soon walked lightly. Moral: Sharing the load from the beginning makes it easier for both.

Explore

Have student partnerships select Aesop fables for independent reading, then partner share the stories (take turns reading to each other). Once they have read the stories, have them use the storyboard planning sheets (activity sheet 1.1) to design the rough drafts of their displays. After they revise and edit their statements and illustration plans, students should use the tagboard panels to create final copies of the display. Remind them to make sure that all the panels face in the same direction when they are attaching them to each other. (*Verbal/Linguistic, Visual/Spatial, and Interpersonal Intelligences*)

Connect

Have students present their fortunately/unfortunately displays to the class. To reinforce the connections between the events of the fable and the moral, discuss this question: What is the connection between the fortunately/unfortunately statements and the morals that conclude the fables?

➤ Activity Plan 5: Creating Original Fables

Materials

Poster showing the characteristics of fables (figure 1.4)
Poster listing the suggested proverbs (figure 1.5)
Activity sheet 1.2, Original Fable Writing (one per student)

Fables	
Length	**Short tales**
Purpose	**Teach lessons**
Characters	**Usually animals; characters are not developed.** **The animals talk and act like human beings.**

➤ Figure 1.4. Characteristics of Fables

Proverbs	
Wishing	Sometimes you wish you had (if you didn't) and wish you hadn't (if you did).
Writing	Don't write before your pencil is sharpened.
Worth	One picture is worth a 1,000 words.
Limits	There's a limit to everything.
Lying	A liar should have a good memory.
Self-reliance	Stand on your own two legs.
Kindness	Kindness brings happiness.
Imagination	Don't let your imagination run away with you.
Help	Three helping each other is as good as six.
Friends	Friends slowly won are long held.

➤ Figure 1.5. Proverbs

An Original Fable: Brainstorming Prewrite	
Moral:	
Character 1:	**Character 2:**
Setting:	
First:	
Next:	
Then:	
Then:	
Then:	
Next:	
End:	
Moral:	

➤Activity Sheet 1.2. Original Fable Writing

Engage

Have students complete this quick think: Start with the number three and use lines to turn it into an animal.

The goal of a quick think is to awaken the brain and have students begin to think in open-ended ways. Students often ask clarification questions about the size of the number, the direction of the number, or the kinds of lines; try not to elaborate and give additional directions, just repeat the first direction and encourage them to imagine what they could do. Some responses may be snakes (bodies), butterflies (wings), camels (humps), rabbits (ears), and owls (eyes). Allow about three minutes of drawing time, then collect and quickly share the drawings. (*Visual/Spatial Intelligence*)

Elaborate

Have students review the characteristics of fables (see figure 1.4), then display the poster to help students keep them in mind.

Have students look at how fables are actually written, keeping the characteristics in mind. The lesson that is learned comes from the events of the story; the moral is closely connected to the actions and responses of the characters in the story. In "The Hippopotamus at Dinner," from *Fables*, the moral is "too much of a good thing often leaves one with a feeling of regret." Have students listen for actions that lead to the lesson that "too much of a good thing often causes regret."

Share the story and analyze it to understand the development of the moral. Have students identify the characters (the Hippo and the waiter) and the setting (Hippo's favorite restaurant), then help list the events of the story that lead to the moral. Ask the students why this moral is wise advice.

THE HIPPOPOTAMUS AT DINNER

1. The Hippo ordered and ate his first meal.

2. It wasn't enough.

3. The Hippo ordered more.

4. He ate his second meal.

5. He felt quite content,

6. until he tried to leave the restaurant.

7. The Hippo couldn't move because his stomach was too fat.

8. The Hippo realized he was stuck,

9. and the Hippo was forlorn (sad).

10. Too much of a good thing leads to trouble.

Explore

Option 1

Review the list of suggested proverbs to make sure students understand what they mean (see figure 1.5).

Option 2

Have students brainstorm a list of human behaviors and create wise sayings about those behaviors. (See figure 1.6 for possibilities.)

Bad behavior	Bad behavior brings bad reactions.
Sharing	If you share even a little, it helps a lot.
Listening	When you listen, you often hear important stuff.
Making mistakes	If you don't learn from your mistakes, you'll keep repeating them.
Greed	If you're greedy, you can't stop even if you've had enough.
Fear	If we can laugh at it, we're usually not afraid.
Talking	If you talk too much, you are not a good doer.

➤ Figure 1.6. Faults

Connect

Have students select proverbs and use the writing process (prewrite, rough draft, revision, editing, publishing) to create original fables. (*Verbal/Linguistic and Visual/Spatial Intelligences*)

Prewriting

Prewriting strategies are the idea-finding activities students pursue in understanding different forms of writing, choosing a topic, collecting details, and developing a writing plan. Students have been building an understanding of fables through listening, reading, and dramatization; now have them use the fable brainstorming chart (activity sheet 1.2) to develop and plan the ideas for their original fables.

Rough Drafting

In rough drafting, students use the information from their prewrite brainstorming to write the first drafts of their stories. Encourage them not to worry about spelling and punctuation and making it perfect, just write and get the ideas of the story on paper.

Revising

Revision activities help students make changes in their rough drafts to improve sequencing, add details or cut information, enhance sentence and paragraph structure, clarify ideas, build imagery, and correct word usage. Fable revisions target sequencing, leads, and use of powerful verbs.

➤ Activity Plan 6: Revision—Sequencing Mini-Lesson

Materials

Supplies for making peanut butter and jelly sandwiches
Small stool or chair

Engage

Make a peanut butter and jelly sandwich in front of the class and use that pattern of actions to introduce the lesson on sequencing. Ask the students: What steps were used in making the sandwich? Why is that process a sequence? Why is a sequence important? (Reinforce this idea of sequence by dramatizing the "Little Miss Muffet" Mother Goose rhyme.) How was sequencing important for the actions of the rhyme? (*Bodily/Kinesthetic Intelligence*)

Elaborate

Share "The Ostrich in Love," from *Fables* (page 21), and ask students to carefully note the sequencing. (It's organized through the days of the week.) Dramatize the actions of the story to emphasize the sequence (*Bodily/Kinesthetic and Logical/Mathematical Intelligences*):

1. What happened first? (On Sunday, Ostrich fell in love and enjoyed following his love from a distance.)

2. What happened next? (On Monday, Ostrich felt joy in leaving her a gift of violets.)

3. Then what happened? (On Tuesday, Ostrich wrote and sang a song for her.)

4. Then? (On Wednesday, Ostrich followed her to a restaurant and was so happy just watching her, he forgot to eat.)

5. Then? (On Thursday, Ostrich was very pleased when he wrote his first poem, even though he was too shy to read it to her.)

6. Then? (On Friday, Ostrich bought himself a new suit of clothes.)

7. Next? (On Saturday, Ostrich experienced a wonderful dream of dancing with his love.)

8. Finally, what happened? (On Sunday, Ostrich realized he was too shy for love, but still felt it was a week well spent.)

9. And the moral is? (Love can be its own reward.)

Explore

Use the moral, "Don't let your imagination run away with you" and the days of the week pattern to create a variation on the story. Variations might focus on one of these ideas: a bump in the night, an unanswered phone call, or a missing red mitten. Keep the moral visible. Ask students to brainstorm characters for the story, then begin imagining the events for each day of the week that will build toward the moral. The bump in the night story might move from a fallen object to a dinosaur wandering into the present from long ago; the unanswered phone call from an advertisement to a long lost friend returning from a trip up the Amazon; the missing red mitten from lost in the attic to being unraveled by birds for a new nest.

A good way to structure the story creation experience is to work together as a class to develop the beginning of the story and brainstorm the first (Monday) event, then divide the class into six groups and have the groups brainstorm six events, encouraging them not to worry about which days of the week they are imagining. For example:

BUMP IN THE NIGHT

Monkey heard a bump in the night and was curious, but then thought it's only a falling branch because the wind is strong tonight. On Monday, he mentioned the bump to Gorilla, who said "That wasn't a falling branch, that was boa exercising her muscles. She squeezed so tightly the tree grew two feet and cracked that boulder as its roots spread across the ground."

AN UNANSWERED PHONE CALL

Mr. and Mrs. Fox were puzzled by phone calls they kept receiving each evening. The phone rang on Sunday, but before they could answer it the phone stopped ringing. On Monday, they had just settled at the table for a delicious dinner when the phone rang; Mr. Fox answered it but all he heard was static. He remarked to Mrs. Fox as he returned to the dinner table, "It must be an advertisement, sometimes advertisers ring a number and play recorded messages. The recording must not be working." On Tuesday, the phone rang again and was answered by Mrs. Fox; all she heard was silence, then the sound of a phone disconnecting. "That's odd," she said to Mr. Fox, "Whoever it was hung up." The rest of the evening they puzzled over the call; they called several friends and relatives but they said they had not made the phone call.

A MISSING RED MITTEN

Cat had a favorite pair of red mittens; she looked forward to wearing them each winter because they kept her warm in the snow and ice. She always stored them carefully away in the cedar chest each spring, but this winter all she could find was one mitten.

"Where could the other mitten be?" she asked herself. On Monday, she had lunch with her friend Tabby and talked about the missing red mitten. Tabby reminded her about the mice living in the attic of her house; maybe they borrowed one mitten for new bedding for the winter.

Cat replied, "How could that be? They aren't strong enough to lift the top of the chest."

When students are ready to share, have each group choose a spokesperson, and as that person shares the group's idea, quickly note the main points on a large card or sheet of typewriter-sized paper. Display the events from the groups and analyze them to create a sequence of daily events that students feel builds toward the moral, "Don't let your imagination run away with you." (*Verbal/ Linguistic and Interpersonal Intelligences*)

Connect

Have students use this heightened awareness of sequencing to revise their original fables for improvements in how the events are developed and sequenced.

➤ Activity Plan 7: Revision—Looking at Leads

Materials

Transparency of Looking at Leads (figure 1.7)

Leads
The purpose of a lead is to ... • **capture attention,** • **draw readers into the story, foreshadow certain events, and** • **create speculation and thinking about how the story will develop.**
Leads can be ... • **surprising/shocking statements,** • **interesting conversations,** • **expressions of feelings,** • **questions or statements of uncertainty, or** • **short descriptions that arouse feelings.**

➤ Figure 1.7. Looking at Leads

Engage

Share the leads listed below and invite students to speculate on the development of the stories from the leads. Ask the students which story they would read first, and why. Ask them how the lead was an effective enticement. (*Verbal/Linguistic Intelligence*)

Lead 1: I crept reluctantly down the endless hallway, shuddering at the horrors in my room! My hand shook as I reached out for the doorknob. I took a deep breath and held it as I shoved open the door.

Lead 2: "Leave me alone!" I shouted at my brother as I stormed into the house and slammed the door behind me.

Lead 3: Looking back at December 25, I can remember every detail, the nods of understanding, the smiles, the looks of encouragement. December 25 was the day my dreams came true.

Elaborate

Share the leads from several fables. Ask the students: What words catch your attention? What questions do you have about how the stories will develop? Use the information in figure 1.7 to remind students of the purposes of and forms for good leads.

Explore

Have students revise their fables to create powerful, interesting leads. As they work on their leads, remind them of these questions:

- Does my lead capture the reader's attention?

- Does my lead draw the reader into the story?

- Does my lead foreshadow later events in the story?

- Does my lead create speculation and thinking about how the story will develop?

Connect

Invite students to take a risk and share their leads. Let students choose whether to ask for suggestions or not; encourage constructive comments and suggestions.

➤ Activity Plan 8: Revision for Powerful Verbs

Materials

Thesaurus dictionaries (one per student partnership)
Small slips of paper listing these words: *gobble, gulp, slurp, dine, devour, chomp, nibble, crunch,* and *devour* (for charades)

Engage

Have students play charades to dramatize verbs that could be substituted for the word *eat.* Student volunteers should draw slips of paper and dramatize the words that are listed; students in the audience must try to guess the words. List the synonyms as they are performed and guessed and reinforce that the dramatized words provide more descriptive images of the word *eat.* (*Bodily/Kinesthetic Intelligence*)

Elaborate

Continue to model revising for more powerful verbs, using the thesaurus dictionaries to locate and discuss substitutes for these words: *talk, choose, lose,* and *run.* (*Verbal/Linguistic Intelligence*)

Explore

Have students use thesaurus dictionaries to revise their fables using stronger verbs. (*Verbal/ Linguistic Intelligence*)

Connect

Have students share and discuss their improvements with partners. (*Interpersonal Intelligence*). They should then go on to editing and publishing.

Editing

Editing is a final step before publishing. In this step students are to address spelling, capitalization, and punctuation corrections.

Publishing

Have students produce handwritten final copies or use a word processing program to publish final copies; they should also illustrate their stories. Plan a sharing day and have students read their stories to the class. To create suspense and audience engagement, have the reader pause and ask students to suggest what they think the moral is before reading it.

2 The Fool of the World and the Flying Ship

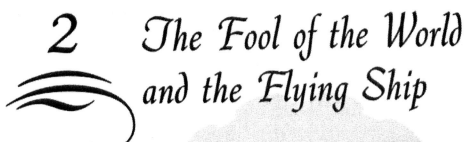

Retold by Arthur Ransome
Illustrated by Uri Shulevitz
New York: Farrar, Straus & Giroux, 1968

Summary

➤ Upon hearing that the czar will give his daughter in marriage to anyone who can bring him a flying ship, the youngest son of an old peasant decides to try, even though he is considered a fool and not very smart. His two brothers set off on their adventure and are never heard from again. The youngest son sets off with his bag over his shoulder and befriends an ancient old man, who rewards him with a flying ship and a warning to offer rides to any people he meets. The youngest son follows the old man's commands and soon arrives at the palace of the czar ready to marry the czar's daughter, only to hear the czar demand completion of three additional tasks.

Award Year

➤ 1969

Art Information

➤ Illustrated using pen and ink and watercolors.

Curriculum Connections

➤ Fairy tales

➤Activity Plan 1: Sharing the Story

Materials

Caldecott Award poster
Pen and ink (available at art stores, or use a fine-point black marker)
Watercolor paint
Drawing paper (small sheets)
Illustrating materials (crayons, markers, paints, colored pencils)

Engage

Have students brainstorm ideas about the word *fool*. Ask them: When someone is thought to be a fool or to act foolishly, what does this mean? As students hear the story, ask them to evaluate whether the youngest son was appropriately named. (*Verbal/Linguistic Intelligence*)

Elaborate

Share the story.

Explore

Ask the students: Is the youngest son a fool? Why or why not? What do you think happened to his two clever older brothers? Of the seven men who joined the youngest son (the listener, the far-shooter, the swift-goer, the eater, the drinker, the man with sticks, and the man with straw), which character was most important to the successful outcome of the story? If you could choose to be one of these characters, which one would it be, and why?

Connect

Ask the students how the setting and the flying ship would change if the story took place in another country. Have them carefully examine the second, double-page illustration showing the ship's arrival at the palace of the czar and focus on how this double-page illustration would look if the story took place in the United States (the president living in the White House), in China (the emperor living in the Imperial Palace), in Alaska (an Eskimo living in an igloo), in the Brazilian rain forest (a scientist living in a tree house), or somewhere else in the world. Three questions must be answered before students begin creating new scenes: Who demands the flying ship, where does this person reside and work, and what changes in design must be made in the flying ship so that it fits the new setting?

Have students work in partnerships to choose new settings, conduct research, prepare preliminary drawings, then complete final copies of the new settings. They should also redesign the flying ships for their settings, bringing in "found" supplies from home to build the redesigned flying ships. For example, the flying ship might look more like Air Force One (the president's plane), a flying bicycle ship for the emperor of China, a flying dog sled for the Eskimo, or a great winged bird for arrival in the rain forest.

Share and display the new settings and place the flying ships in the foregrounds of the settings. (*Visual/Spatial and Interpersonal Intelligences*)

Share the Caldecott Award information:

1. As students examine the cover of the book, ask them what special thing they notice. (gold medal) Ask them what the name of the medal is. (Caldecott Award Medal) Ask them why it has been placed on this book. (Some answers may be: The illustrations are special, well done, particularly interesting, exciting, and/or unusual.)

2. Discuss the art techniques used in creating the pictures. Pen and ink provides the framework for each illustration, and it would be interesting to know whether the pen and ink was used first or after the color applications. (Slowly browse the book to look at the use of pen and ink; in some illustrations I think the pen and ink was used first and the color added, but some of the lines drawn on the clothing make me think the color was applied first and pen and ink used second to outline and add detail.) The stand of trees on the page where the fool receives the flying ship (he's lying on the ground with an ax beside him) really shows the pen-and-ink application.

    Ask the students what media were used to add color to the illustrations. (watercolor paints) Ask them how the illustrations help us know that the story is a Russian tale. (clothing worn by the characters and the architecture of the palace of the czar)

3. Ask two student volunteers to search the poster for the year the story won. (Searching the poster helps students become familiar with the many different titles selected for the award.)

➤ Activity Plan 2: Semantic Webbing

Materials

Multiple copies of the book (one for each small group)

Note: Help students map the story to develop understanding of the setting, characters, conflict, plot development, and theme. This kind of webbing (see figure 2.1) helps students see important characteristics of the story, increases understanding of the structure of fairy tales, and connects and bears fruit in their own creative writing. Gather enough copies of the story so students can work in small groups during the activity.

Engage

Start with the setting and brainstorm words and phrases that identify the setting; encourage students to use the book as you brainstorm.

Elaborate

Continue with characters and have the students list two or three important characters, describing their characteristics, again referring to the book to add details.

Explore

Plot development is the next task; students should focus on beginning, middle, and end important events.

Connect

Conflict and theme portions of the web will be more challenging for the students and may require considerable discussion. The following questions may help in the discussion: What is the message of the story? Why does the fool succeed? Where are the problem areas? (*Visual/Spatial and Verbal/Linguistic Intelligences*)

➤ Activity Plan 3: Which Character Are You?

Materials

Large sheets of white butcher paper, cut long enough so a student's body outline can be traced on the paper
Illustrating materials (crayons, markers, paints, colored pencils)

Engage

List the characters from the story (the listener, the far-seer, the swift-goer, the eater, the drinker, the man with sticks, and the man with straw) and ask the students to describe their abilities. (*Logical/Mathematical Intelligence*)

Elaborate

Discuss how these abilities might be helpful today. Be sure to remind students to focus on positive, helpful ideas. Refocus questions: In what career or situation might the far-seeing ability be useful? (forest ranger, ocean salvage expert, miner) How might the straw be useful? (cure for a drought, ice cubes at the touch of a hand) Who would use the skills of the listener? (earthquake and volcano warnings, spies) How would the drinker be helpful in a community? (flood prevention) How would the skills of the swift-goer be used? (delivery person, post office employee, pinch runner in a baseball game) What would be the job of a modern-day eater or the man with the sticks? (food taster or armed forces recruiter)

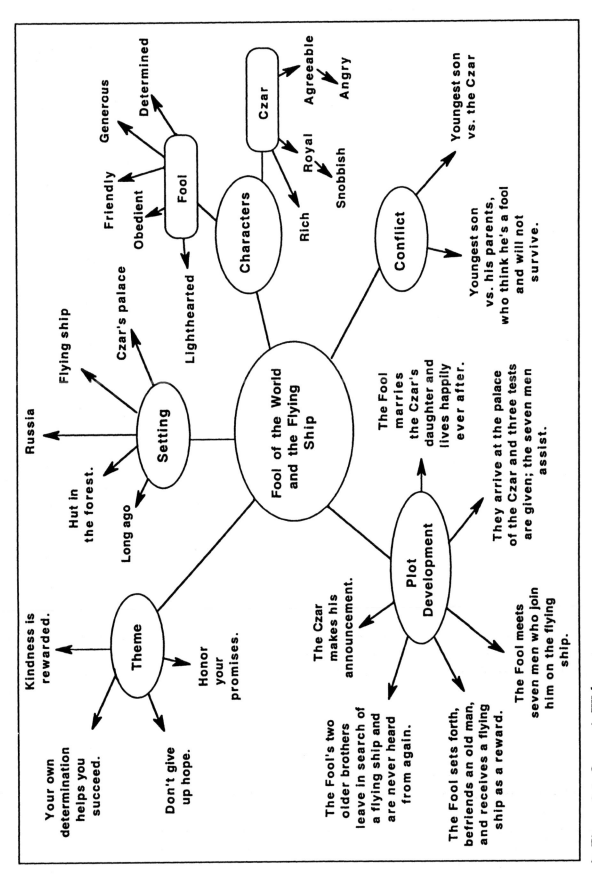

► Figure 2.1. Semantic Web

Explore

Have students work in partnerships to choose characters and use large sheets of paper to trace around one partner's body. Students should decorate the figures so they show modern-day applications of the abilities of the characters and should create description plaques explaining how the abilities are used. For example, if the figure were the swift-goer and the swift-goer played soccer, football, or baseball, the figure would be dressed in clothes appropriate for the chosen sport and the description would explain exciting plays completed by the swift-goer's speedy abilities. (*Visual/Spatial, Interpersonal, and Verbal/Linguistic Intelligences*)

Connect

Display the gallery of characters and let students browse and read the descriptions of modern-day applications for the abilities of the seven men.

➤ Activity Plan 4: Characters, Revisited

Materials

Activity sheet 2.1, Characterization Web (one per student)
The Fairy Tale Cookbook by Carol MacGregor (New York: Macmillan, 1982)
Tea party supplies

Engage

There are many other interesting and memorable characters from fairy tales. Choose a character to impersonate and begin the lesson as that character, talking and acting in character. Easy characters to impersonate are Little Red Riding Hood (wear a red cape, a red hooded sweatshirt or a red jacket and knitted cap, and carry a basket) or Puss in Boots (dress in a dark turtleneck and matching slacks and wear boots and a big hat). Little Red Riding Hood would skip and sing and discuss her sick grandmother; Puss in Boots would meow, make washing movements, and talk about his plans for bringing wealth to the miller's son. (*Bodily/Kinesthetic Intelligence*)

Elaborate

Use your impersonation to model the characterization web and help students understand how to use the information to write riddles and dress and act as fairy tale characters.

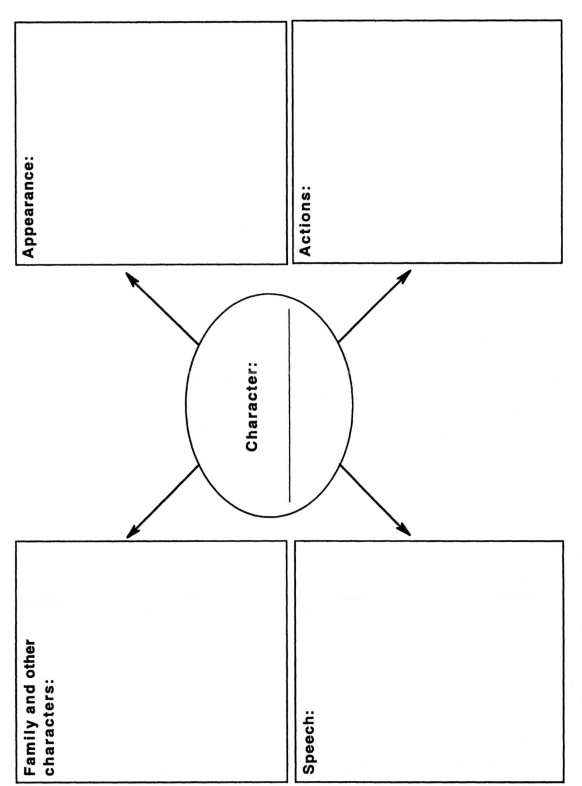

Appearance:

Actions:

Character:

Family and other characters:

Speech:

► Activity Sheet 2.1. Characterization Web

The characterization web for Puss in Boots might show this information:

- Family and other characters: youngest son (Marquis of Carabas), king, king's daughter, ogre

- Appearance: boots, bag, hunter's hat, characteristics of a cat

- Actions: arching back, washing motions, stalking and pouncing motions (clever at catching rats and mice, caught a rabbit and two partridges for the king), puffed with pride, tricked an ogre

- Speech: meow, purr, scratchy voice

Riddles might be:

Riddle

I was a gift to a youngest son.
I caught a rabbit and two partridges for the king.
Because of me the youngest son became the Marquis of Carabas
and mowers and reapers claimed to work for him.
My greatest accomplishment was to trick the ogre into becoming a mouse.
When he did that I ate him!
I love my boots!
Who am I?
(Puss in Boots)

Riddle

I picked flowers and skipped and sang,
then stopped to visit with a stranger,
which caused all the trouble.
I knew something wasn't right
when I saw grandma's eyes and ears.
Luckily, the woodcutter heard my cries for help
and rescued us, so . . .
I can still wear my famous red cape.
Who am I?
(Little Red Riding Hood)

Explore

Have students select fairy tale characters and complete characterization webs (activity sheet 2.1), then write riddles about the characters. (*Verbal/Linguistic Intelligence*)

Connect

Have students work with each other to rehearse their characterizations and gain practice talking and acting as the characters.

Plan a fairy tale tea party to celebrate character investigations. Have students come dressed as their characters and act and converse as the characters. Display setting variation pictures (activity from the introductory lesson) and have students dramatically share their riddles.

Serve foods from *The Fairy Tale Cookbook.* Decorating gingerbread cookies is a fun activity for the party. Bake the cookies ahead of time and gather decorating supplies: frosting, small candies (Lifesavers, gumdrops, gummy bears, etc.). An easy variation on the recipe can be done by skipping step one and making a change after step five. Instead of rolling out the dough, drop rounded tablespoons of the cookie dough onto baking sheets, press flat with the bottom of a buttered, sugared glass, and bake eight to ten minutes or until lightly browned.

3 Lon Po Po: A Red-Riding Hood Story from China

Translated by Ed Young
Illustrated by Ed Young
New York: Philomel Books, 1989

Summary

➤ Shang, Tao, and Paotze are home alone because their mother has gone to visit their grandmother. She has warned them to close the door tight and latch it well. Shortly after she leaves, a wolf disguised as their grandmother appears at the door and quickly convinces the two younger sisters to open the door. Shang is not so easily fooled, discovers the true identity of the wolf, and devises a plan to save herself and her sisters.

Award Year

➤ 1990

Art Information

➤ Illustrated using ancient Chinese panel art techniques, watercolors, and pastels.

Curriculum Connections

➤ Fairy tales

➤Activity Plan 1: Sharing the Story

Materials

Three "feel" bags—one filled with synthetic fur, one with something sharp such as a
thorn, and one with some type of nut such as walnuts
Caldecott Award poster
Watercolor paint (available at art supply stores)
Pastel crayon (available at art supply stores)
Paintbrush
Small cup of water

Engage

Divide the class into three groups and give each group one of the "feel" bags. Have students feel the objects without looking and brainstorm words that describe the touch of the objects, then try to name the objects. Have each group share descriptive words and conclusions developed from the descriptive words. Were students fooled? Why or why not? (*Bodily/Kinesthetic and Verbal/Linguistic Intelligences*)

Elaborate

Divide the class in half and dramatize the conversation between the wolf and Little Red Riding Hood from the familiar version of Little Red Riding Hood by the Brothers Grimm. (*Verbal/Linguistic Intelligence*)

Little Red Riding Hood	The Wolf
"Grandmama, what great ears you have!"	"All the better to hear you, my dear!"
"Grandmama, what great eyes you have!"	"All the better to see you, my dear!"
"Grandmama, what great arms you have!"	"All the better to hug you, my dear!"
"Grandmama, what great teeth you have!"	"All the better to eat you, my dear!"

Remind students that this conversation comes from the traditional story of Little Red Riding Hood and that you will be sharing a Chinese version of the story. Ask students to notice similarities and differences as they listen to the story. Pause on the page where Shang lights the light and discovers the wolf's true identity.

Explore

Use the creative problem-solving process to have students create solutions to the problem the three sisters face. (*Logical/Mathematical Intelligence*)

Sensing the Problem

Shang knew that the visitor was trouble after she lit the light and saw the wolf's face.

Fact Finding

Determine the available facts in the story to this point (who, what, where, when, why, how). Students should list some of the following ideas:

Three sisters are alone at home because their mother has gone to visit their grandmother.

She warned them to close the door at sunset and latch it well; however, they are tricked by a wolf disguised as their Po Po.

Shang is resourceful and clever and has discovered the presence of the wolf, and is determined to save her sisters.

There are three of them and only one wolf; they are familiar with the house and the land surrounding the house and the wolf is not as familiar.

Problem Finding

Have the students restate the problem in at least three ways and decide which statement most accurately defines the problem in the story. Problem statements begin with "How might . . ." and continue with one active verb and any qualifying conditions. For example, how might Shang and her sisters get rid of the wolf and save themselves before their mother returns?

Idea Finding

Have students work in small groups to brainstorm solutions to the problem of the wolf. One student should act as recorder in each group. (*Interpersonal Intelligence*)

Solution Finding

Use chart paper, the chalkboard, or the overhead projector and set up the problem-solving grid (see figure 3.1). List the criteria for judging the solutions across the top of the grid and list the solutions down the side of the grid. Students should come up with the criteria, but ideas you might expect include the following: The girls use materials and resources from their home or land, the wolf is fooled, the wolf is gone, and it happens before mother returns. Rate the solution ideas from one to five (five means that the solution effectively meets that criterion, one means that the solution does not meet the criterion) for each criterion and determine which solution seems to work most effectively.

Story ideas from the student groups	Uses available materials	The wolf is fooled	The wolf is gone	Happens before mother returns
Group 1				
Group 2				
Group 3				
Group 4				

➤ Figure 3.1. Creative Problem-Solving Solution Grid

Connect

Share the end of the story as written by Mr. Young and compare his solution with the students' most effective solution.

Discuss the similarities and differences between this version and the traditional story of Little Red Riding Hood.

Share the Caldecott Award information:

1. As students examine the cover of the book, ask them what special thing they notice. (gold medal) Ask them what the name of the medal is. (Caldecott Award Medal) Ask them why it has been placed on this book. (Some answers may be: The illustrations are special, well done, particularly interesting, exciting, and/or unusual.)

2. Discuss the art techniques used in creating the pictures. Slowly browse the book again and ask students to comment on the structure of the illustrations. As you turn each page, ask students what they notice about how the art is arranged on the page. (Except for a few pages near the end of the story, the double-page illustrations are all one picture, but broken into panels, as though Mr. Young painted one picture, then cut and framed it into three sections.)

    Ask students what media were used to add color to the illustrations. (Browse the illustrations and have students speculate.) Watercolor and pastels provide the color; they create a soft, dreamlike backdrop that makes certain features of the children and the wolf (the eyes and teeth, particularly) stand out. (Use a sheet of drawing paper to demonstrate the look of the pastel crayons and the watercolor paint.)

3. Ask two student volunteers to search the poster for the year the story won. (Searching the poster helps students become familiar with the many different titles selected for the award.)

➤ Activity Plan 2: Comparing Wolf Stories

Materials

Wolf story variations:

- *Little Red Cowboy Hat* by Susan Lowell, illustrated by Randy Cecil (New York: Henry Holt, 1997). Little Red sets off for her grandmother's ranch carrying a loaf of bread and a jar of jelly; she hasn't traveled far when she stops to pick some flowers and encounters a wolf.

- *Little Red Riding Hood* by Lisa Campbell Ernst, illustrated by Lisa Campbell Ernst (New York: Simon & Schuster, 1995). Little Red Riding Hood aired up the tires on her bike, tested the brakes, settled the basket of muffins and lemonade on the handlebars, and set off to Grandma's; she had not traveled far when a wolf leapt into her path.

- *The Wolf and the Seven Little Kids* by the Brothers Grimm, illustrated by Felix Hoffmann (New York: Harcourt, Brace & World, 1957). When she has to leave them to fetch something from the forest, Mother Goat warns her seven little kids of the dangers of the wolf. Shortly after she leaves, the wolf appears and tries to trick the kids with his voice, but they are not fooled; he tries again but they ask to see his paws and are not tricked because the paws are black. However, when the wolf flours his paws, they are fooled, open the door, and all are swallowed except the youngest.

- *Peter and the Wolf* retold and illustrated by Ian Beck (New York: Atheneum, 1995). Peter opens the garden gate to walk into the meadow and see his friend bird; duck follows and makes straight for the pond. When Grandfather sees that Peter has left the gate open and gone into the meadow alone, he is angry; he warns Peter about the dangers of the wolf and brings him home again. Soon after, a wolf slinks out of the forest and Peter's adventures begin again.

Activity sheet 3.1, Comparison Chart (one per student partnership)

Engage

Reprise the conversation between Little Red Riding Hood and the wolf. (*Verbal/Linguistic Intelligence*)

Elaborate

Work with the students to complete a comparison chart on *Lon Po Po*, including country of origin, setting, characters, problem, actions, and resolution.

Story:
Country of Origin:
Setting (where/when):
Characters:
Problem:
Actions:
Resolution:

➤Activity Sheet 3.1. Comparison Chart

LON PO PO

Country of origin: China

Setting (where and when): In the country; long, long ago

Characters: Shang, Tao, Paotze (three sisters); mother; wolf

Problem: The children are fooled by a wolf when their mother leaves them alone to visit their grandmother.

Actions:

Action 1. Mother leaves and warns the children to lock the door.

Action 2. The wolf comes and tricks the children.

Action 3. The children begin to notice unusual characteristics of their Po Po: the wolf's tail (your foot has a bush on it) and the wolf's sharp claws (your hand has thorns on it).

Action 4. Shang lights the lamp and discovers the truth.

Action 5. Shang and her sisters use desire for the ginkgo tree's fruit to trick the wolf.

Action 6. The wolf breaks his heart and the children are safe.

Resolution: Mother returns with baskets of food from the real Po Po.

Explore

Divide students into small groups and have them read the variants and prepare comparison charts, using activity sheet 3.1. (*Interpersonal, Verbal/Linguistic, Logical/Mathematical, and Visual/Spatial Intelligences*)

Connect

When the charts are completed, display them in a row and discuss the similarities and differences. Ask the students: Which variants are most like the traditional version? Which are very different?

➤ Activity Plan 3: Exploring Panel Art

Materials

Wolf story variants (see the stories listed in Activity Plan 2)
Completed comparison charts (from Activity Plan 2)
Large sheets of white drawing paper (at least 11 x 17 inches)
Large construction paper sheets in a variety of colors (larger than the white drawing paper)
Scissors
Illustrating materials (watercolors, brushes, colored pencils, and markers)

Engage

Mr. Young used Chinese panel art techniques to illustrate *Lon Po Po*. Look at the book again and closely examine the pictures so students understand the panel art technique. (Each panel art display is actually one continuous picture that has been divided into halves, thirds, or fourths.)

Elaborate

Have students return to their wolf variant groups to review the comparison charts and select assignments, setting, characters, actions, or the resolution, then discuss how they will illustrate the assignments.

Explore

Once the assignments are chosen and discussed, have students follow this design process (figure 3.2 shows examples of the steps):

1. Make a rough sketch to plan the drawing that illustrates the assignment.

2. Analyze the rough sketch to decide how it could be divided into three panels; draw the dividing lines. (Note that the drawing does not have to be divided into three equal panels.)

3. Use the large drawing paper, watercolors, and colored pencils to create the final illustration.

4. When it is dry, cut the illustration into three panels and carefully paste each panel onto a construction paper background (allow a half inch of space between each panel).

5. Use a marker to create a frame around each panel. (*Visual/Spatial Intelligence*)

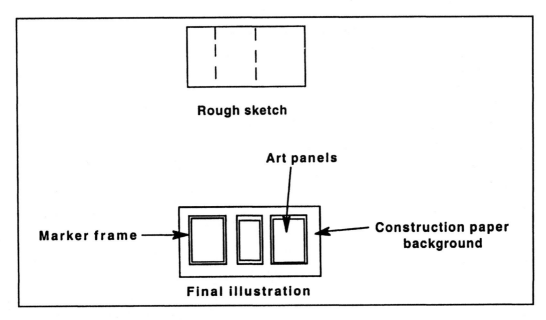

➤Figure 3.2. Panel Art Display

Connect

Display and share the panel art pictures.

➤Activity Plan 4: What a Reputation!

Materials

Chart paper
Research session in the library (Schedule time in the library so students can investigate the habits of wolves.)

Engage

Address the students as follows:

Imagine . . . [pause until you have the students' attention] winter night, full moon turning the landscape ghostly, trees spreading bare arms, creaking in the wind. Silence . . . silence . . . suddenly the eerie howl of a wolf breaks the winter silence. Goose bumps, shivers. Fear flows as we imagine all the legends and stories about the big bad wolf.

Elaborate

Discuss these questions with the students: Does the wolf deserve this reputation? Is the wolf sly, sneaky, and just plain mean?

Explore

Continue this investigation. Create a two-column chart labeled "Yes, the wolf deserves this reputation" and "No, the wolf doesn't deserve this reputation" (see figure 3.3). Have students research information about the wolf and use their research information to take a stance and contribute an opinion and illustration to the chart.

For example:

> No, wolves don't deserve this reputation because they are actually quite friendly with each other. They live in packs, usually five to eight wolves together, and hunt, travel, eat, and make noises together. They also baby-sit each other's litters.

The picture for this opinion shows wolves playing together in a pack.

Another example:

> No, wolves don't deserve this reputation even though their howling is scary. Wolves howl in the day and the night to call the pack together for the hunt, to locate each other, and sometimes just for the fun of it. They seem to howl more frequently during the winter; the howling sounds really carry in the winter, and this is why it seems so scary.

The picture of this opinion shows a wolf howling in the moonlit night.

An example for the "bad" reputation side might say:

> Yes, wolves deserve this reputation because if you watch them hunt a moose it's ferocious. They hunt in packs and surround the moose; one wolf tears at the head of the moose and the others jump at the sides and stomach.

The picture shows a moose surrounded by wolves.

Connect

Review the chart and draw conclusions about the truth of the wolf's reputation.

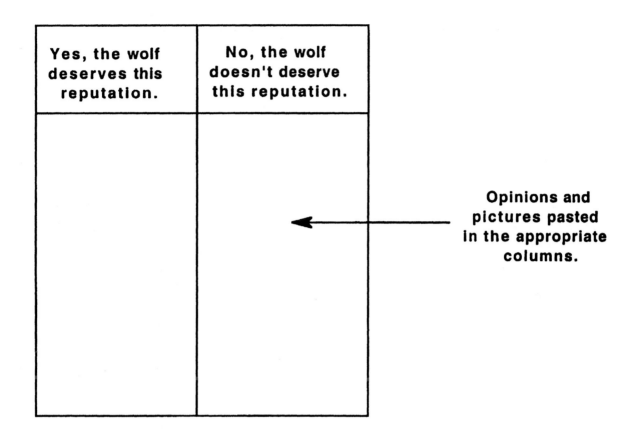

Yes, the wolf deserves this reputation.	No, the wolf doesn't deserve this reputation.

Opinions and pictures pasted in the appropriate columns.

➤ Figure 3.3. Wolf Opinion Chart

4 Mirette on the High Wire

Written by Emily Arnold McCully
Illustrated by Emily Arnold McCully
New York: Putnam, 1992

Summary

➤ When Monsieur Bellini comes to stay in her mother's boardinghouse on English Street, Mirette is fascinated by his abilities on the high wire and begs him to teach her. In mentoring Mirette, Monsieur Bellini regains his own courage on the wire.

Award Year

➤ 1993

Art Information

➤ Illustrated using watercolors.

Curriculum Connections

➤ Characters

➤Activity Plan 1: Sharing the Story

Materials

Masking tape
Watercolor pigment (available at art supply stores)
Paintbrush (available at art supply stores)
Caldecott Award poster

Engage

For fun, begin with these balancing movements:

1. Have students stand on one leg with arms held tightly at their sides, then repeat the movement, but this time using their arms to add balance and stability. Ask them how balance and stability improve.

2. Mark the floor with two parallel strips of masking tape, measuring eight to ten feet in length and spaced about three inches apart (see figure 4.1). Ask students to walk between the lines, one foot in front of the other, while they are watching their feet, then repeat the movement, but this time looking straight ahead at a fixed point. Ask the students how the change in focal point (where your eyes focus) improves the ease and speed of movement. (*Bodily/Kinesthetic Intelligence*)

➤ Figure 4.1. Masking Tape Lines

Elaborate

Introduce the students to the story as follows:

Movement and balance are important elements of the story we will share today. In the story we are introduced to Monsieur Bellini, the high-wire artist; he walks a thin wire high above the audience's head. As you think about this job, what do you think would be your greatest challenges? (Record students' responses, then share the story.)

Explore

Discuss the story as follows:

What was Monsieur Bellini's greatest challenge? [fear] What do you think caused the fear? From the first moment Mirette saw Monsieur Bellini walking the wire, she was enchanted and "her feet tingled, as if they wanted to jump up on the wire" beside him. What sparked this intense interest on Mirette's part? How do you think she will avoid the fear that troubled Bellini? How do you interpret the closing picture?

Have students think about times in their lives when they were determined to learn something new (like Mirette). Ask them what challenges they faced and how they felt when they mastered the new skill. Ask them what they learned about themselves through the process. Let them think for a while, then have students share and discuss with partners. (*Intrapersonal and Interpersonal Intelligences*)

Connect

Share the Caldecott Award information:

1. As students examine the cover of the book, ask them what special thing they notice. (gold medal) Ask them what the name of the medal is. (Caldecott Award Medal) Ask them why it has been placed on this book. (Some answers may be: The illustrations are special, well done, particularly interesting, exciting, and/or unusual.)

2. Discuss the art techniques used in creating the pictures. The watercolor illustrations really capture the vibrancy and variety of life in the boardinghouse on English Street. Browse the illustrations once again, commenting on the colors and textures: The sheen of the copper pot and the costumes of the guests on the opening pages of the story build confirmation that the boardinghouse is a colorful, exciting place to live and work; on the fifth page of the story, the reader can almost feel the wind billowing the sheets and mirror Mirette's awed stance as she glimpses Bellini on the high wire for the first time; the muted backgrounds found on the pages where Mirette attempts the high wire herself quietly focus the reader's attention on Mirette's struggle to walk its length and show Bellini she is determined to learn the high wire; the pages illustrating the agent's stories of Bellini's accomplishments (cooking the omelet high above Niagara Falls and firing a cannon over the bullring in Barcelona) strongly reinforce the daring and excitement of his work; and finally, on the pages showing Bellini's great walk, the nighttime sky, the dulled colors of the rooftops, and the light on the wire create suspense and anticipation.

3. Ask two student volunteers to search the poster for the year the story won. (Searching the poster helps students become familiar with the many different titles selected for the award.)

➤Activity Plan 2: Notable Characters

Materials

Novels for independent reading (Make arrangements with the media specialist to booktalk a selection of novel titles featuring strong and interesting characters.)

A memorable character from children's literature (Select a character from children's literature whom you have really enjoyed and feel is memorable and develop reasons for your choice. For example, I've always liked the character of Peter in the stories of Ezra Jack Keats because he seems so human and natural; he enjoys dragging a stick through the snow just for the fun of it and he's curious about how long a snowball will last indoors [*The Snowy Day*, 1962]; he's triumphant and feels a wonderful sense of accomplishment when he finally learns to whistle [*Whistle for Willie*, 1964]; the arrival of a baby sister brings jealousy and a feeling of displacement until he realizes that he really has outgrown his baby furniture [*Peter's Chair*, 1967]; he loves and values his friends, enjoying escapades with Archie, his best friend [*Goggles*, 1969 and *Hi Cat*, 1970], and deciding to invite a girl to his birthday [*A Letter to Amy*, 1968].)

Writing journals (In "Living Like a Writer," writing journals are the notebooks students carry with them, constantly recording ideas such as responses to and descriptions of things they see and experience, interesting words, flashes of imagination, "what if" speculations, and connections sparked by books, speakers, and films; writing journals can also hold meaningful photographs, lists, sketches, newspaper clippings, ticket stubs, and other memorabilia—anything that provides seeds for writing. Spiral notebooks work well as writing journals; encourage students to use these journals exclusively for writing and to resist tearing pages from the journals for other uses.)

Engage

Share your memorable character and invite students to think about books they have read and characters they identify as memorable. As they think of these characters, have students use their writing journals to record words and phrases explaining why they are memorable. Circulate and encourage students to work independently; in a moment they will have an opportunity to share in pairs or small groups. Some questions to ask if students are stumped are: What do you like/dislike about the character? How are you similar to or different from the character? When you selected this character, what ideas first popped into your head? What word(s) capture(s) the personality of the character? (*Verbal/Linguistic Intelligence*)

Elaborate

Have students gather in pairs or small groups to share their character selections and reasons. Set the following goals for their collaborations: Each member should have an opportunity to share; the discussion should give the group time to compare reasons, generate additional reasons, and draw conclusions about characteristics of memorable characters in literature; and one student should record and be prepared to share the conclusions of the group. (*Interpersonal Intelligence*)

Explore

Have collaborative groups share their ideas (record the ideas on chart paper or the board) and begin a class discussion on how authors develop these characters we like. Ask the students: How does the author make the reader really care about the character? How has the author made the character believable? (Describing the character, sharing the character's conversations and thoughts and actions, and showing the way others view the character are all strategies authors use to build real characters.) Tell the students that when an author really develops characters and makes them believable and "true to life," we say the author has developed a "round" character. "Flat" characters are not fully developed in stories.

Connect

Have students listen to the book talk presented by the media specialist or browse in the library for good "character" chapter books. Also, select one book as a read-aloud.

On returning to the classroom, have the students set a schedule for reading. Provide sustained silent reading time during school hours and encourage students to set at-home reading goals. Once reading goals are set, pose thinking questions to help students apply the "memorable characters" discussion and have them read the first chapters of their books. Ask them to think about these questions: Which character will be a round character? How does the author make this character believable? Refocus questions: Which character will be the center of the story? How does the author introduce the character?

➤ Activity Plan 3: Protagonist/Antagonist

Materials

Mirette on the High Wire by Emily Arnold McCully

A selection of easy picture books (Work with the media specialist to select a variety of picture books that provide models of the types of characters: protagonist, antagonist, dynamic and static characters.)

Engage

Revisit the story of Mirette and have students recall and list the characters in the story (Mirette, Monsieur Bellini, Madame Gateau, the guests of the boardinghouse, the agent from the Hippodrome).

Elaborate

Discuss the characters using the following questions:

1. Which character do you identify with most? Why? (Answers and reasons will vary.)

2. What would you identify as the problem of the story? (Monsieur Bellini cannot perform on the high wire and has retired because he is afraid on the wire and cannot get rid of his fear.)

3. Which characters are involved in the problem? (Mirette, Monsieur Bellini, the agent)

4. Which character is central to the problem? (Monsieur Bellini) (On the board, write *protagonist* next to Monsieur Bellini's name and explain that Monsieur Bellini is called the protagonist because without him the problem would not exist.)

5. Who is another character who is significant for the problem? (Mirette) (On the board, write *antagonist* next to Mirette's name and explain that Mirette is called the antagonist of the story because the problem could not develop without Mirette's presence.)

6. When I think of the relationship between the protagonist and the antagonist, I think of words like *action/reaction* and *equilibrium/disequilibrium* and movements like the give and take of a tug-of-war. How is Mirette a force that struggles against the protagonist? (She won't let Monsieur Bellini give up. First, she convinces him to teach her how to walk the wire, then her disappointment is instrumental in making him decide to try again, and finally, when he freezes on the wire, she joins him, breaking the grip of his fear.)

7. There are other ways to think of characters in a story. Which character changes during the story? (Monsieur Bellini) How? A character who experiences change in a story is called a *dynamic* character. Monsieur Bellini overcomes his fear of the wire and is able to return to performing by the end of the story.

8. Which character doesn't really change in the story? (Mirette) A character who doesn't experience change in a story is called a *static* character. Mirette is a static character; although she learns to walk the wire, her personality doesn't really change.

Explore

Continue developing understanding of types of characters. Have students work with partners to select easy picture books, identify the four types of characters in their stories (protagonist, antagonist, dynamic character, and static character), and use art supplies to create the characters. Have students include evidence that supports their identifications of the characters. (*Interpersonal and Visual/Spatial Intelligences*)

Connect

Share characters and have students discuss and ask questions about each story.

➤ Activity Plan 4: Notable Characters Revisited

Materials

Transparency of the character sketch about Jonathan (figure 4.2)
Transparency and multiple copies of activity sheet 4.1, Character Sketch Prewrite
    Brainstorming, Option 1
Transparency and multiple copies of activity sheet 4.2, Character Sketch Prewrite
    Brainstorming, Option 2
Writing journals

Engage

Draw a circle and a line on the board; write *round* below the circle and *flat* below the line (see figure 4.3). Have students review ideas about round and flat characters and add their comments to the board.

Elaborate

Display the transparency and share the character description paragraph describing Jonathan (see figure 4.2). Read it slowly and encourage students to build a mental picture of Jonathan. Some students may wish to sketch as you read. Ask the students what words of the writer really helped them see the character.

Explore

Tell the students that you want to explore developing a character sketch of one of the characters in the read-aloud to get a closer look at how writers develop characters.

Use the transparency of activity sheet 4.1 to model one example. Ask the students: As you think about the story and the character of (choose a character from the read-aloud), how would you describe his or her personality? (Personality traits may include outgoing, determined, courageous, sensitive, changeable, funny, grown-up, or wise.) Select one idea and ask students to think of examples from the read-aloud that provide evidence that the character has that personality trait.

Use the transparency of activity sheet 4.2 to model another example. Ask the students which words from the story they would place in each box (appearance, speech, feelings/emotions, actions).

Connect

Have students select one of the character sketch brainstorming sheets, choose characters from their own books, and begin to add ideas for their own character sketches. (*Verbal/Linguistic Intelligence*)

Text continues on page 57.

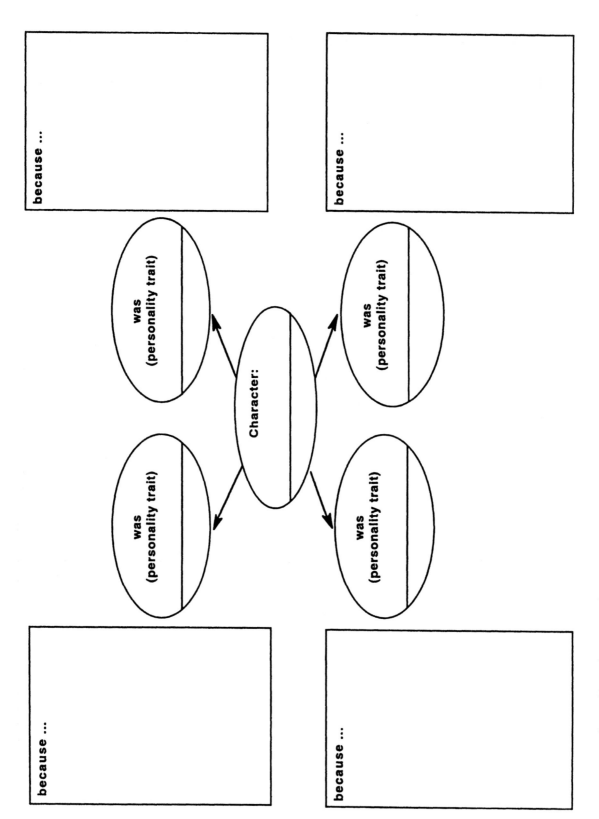

▶ Activity Sheet 4.1. Character Sketch Prewrite Brainstorming, Option 1

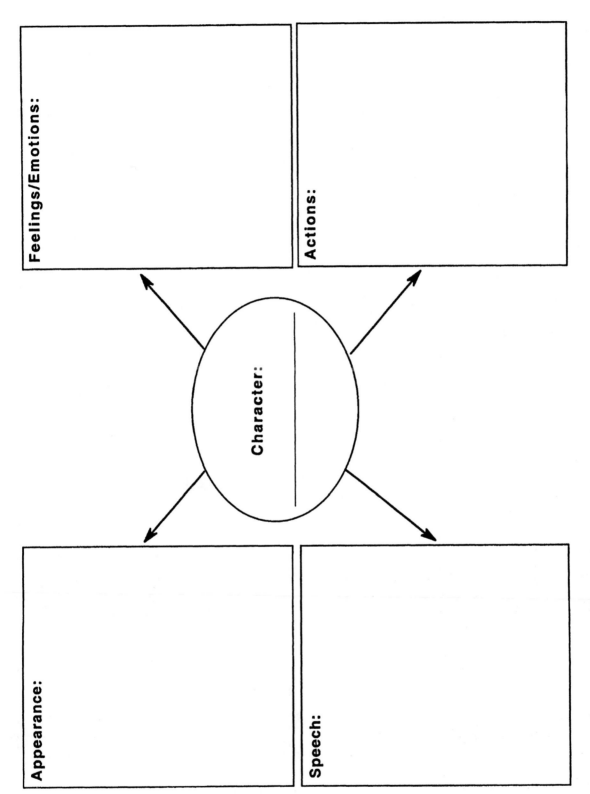

Feelings/Emotions:

Actions:

Character:

Appearance:

Speech:

► Activity Sheet 4.2. Character Sketch Prewrite Brainstorming, Option 2

Character Sketch: Jonathan

I felt I already knew a lot about Jonathan, just by watching his face. The first thing I observed were his eyes, they were big and blue with a special twinkle of excitement and expectation as he stood in the on-deck circle, slowly swinging his bat. I saw his look of concentration as he studied the pitcher's wind-up and delivery, preparing himself for his turn at bat. I wouldn't have noticed his nose, except it was covered in white, protecting it from the glare of the afternoon sun. His mouth was a thin line of determination as he walked to the plate and got ready for the first pitch.

"Strike!" yelled the umpire. Jonathan gritted his teeth in renewed determination, the crowd quieted, the pitcher nodded his head, once, twice, then began his windup and delivery. I'll never forget his smile of triumph when Jonathan connected with the ball and headed for first. As he removed his batting glove and listened to the advice of the first-base coach, his faced showed his self-confidence.

➤ Figure 4.2. Character Sketch: Jonathan

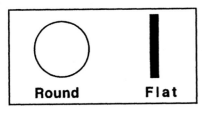

➤ Figure 4.3. Round/Flat Characters

➤ Activity Plan 5: Writing the Character Sketches

Materials

Transparency of the character sketch about Ramona (figure 4.4)
Transparency of topic sentences (figure 4.5)
Transparency of questions for supporting detail sentences (figure 4.6)
Transparency of closing sentence examples (figure 4.7)
Selection of character descriptions for read-alouds (Try the following: from *James and the Giant Peach* by Roald Dahl (New York: Knopf, 1961), the paragraph on page 6 describing Aunt Sponge and Aunt Spiker; from *Ramona the Brave* by Beverly Cleary (New York: William Morrow, 1975), on pages 19–20, Ramona's description of herself; from *Shiloh* by Phyllis Reynolds Naylor (New York: Atheneum, 1991), on pages 13–15, Marty's description of his first encounter with the dog, Shiloh; from *Mrs. Frisby and the Rats of NIMH* by Robert C. O'Brien (New York: Atheneum, 1971), the second paragraph on page 21, Mrs. Frisby's description of the cat called Dragon.)

Engage

Display and share the character sketch about Ramona (see figure 4.4). This is another example of the type of character sketch students will be writing, about one of the characters from their books. Share other examples from the novels you have selected.

Elaborate

Use the transparency of the topic sentence examples (figure 4.5) to introduce the structure of a paragraph as follows:

1. The *topic sentence* begins the sketch and introduces the character. It has two parts: a subject and a focus. The subject tells the who or what, and the focus shares a feeling or attitude or perspective about the subject. In the sketch about Ramona, Ramona is the subject. What is the focus of the sketch?

Character Sketch: Ramona

Now that the first day of third grade had arrived, Ramona felt "tall, grown-up, and sort of ... well, wise in the ways of the world." Even though her stomach felt quivery, she was determined not to get carsick on the bus ride and made herself think, instead, about the pleasure of attending a new school where none of her teachers would know she was Beatrice's little sister. She ignored Howie's comment about her big feet and said to herself, "Why shouldn't my new sandals make my feet look big; my feet have grown since my last pair." When she realized that she had dropped her new pink eraser and Danny had taken it and refused to return it, she carefully planned her strategy for getting it back, deciding that name-calling and anger weren't good choices. Much to her surprise, an opportunity came soon after class began when Ms. Whaley asked her to distribute paper for nametags. As she passed Danny's desk and gave him a slip of paper, she whispered in her most convincing voice, "You give me back my eraser!"

Danny whispered back, "Try and get it, Bigfoot."

Ramona stared at her feet, trying to think of a good comeback. "Superfoot to you," she finally replied and much to her amazement, Danny pulled her eraser out of his pocket and handed it to her with a grin.   Ramona was happy as she returned to her desk. She liked feeling tall in her new school and even though Danny was a problem, so far she had not let him get the best of her for keeps.

➤ Figure 4.4. Character Sketch: Ramona

Look at other examples and identify the subject and focus of each topic sentence. Refocus questions: What will be the topic of the sketch? What is the purpose of the sketch?

- Subject: Melissa
  Focus: Showing how she is confident as a latchkey kid.

- Subject: Marcus
  Focus: Giving examples of his shyness.

- Subject: Grandma
  Focus: Showing how she is adventurous.

- Subject: The friendship between Jeff and Megan
  Focus: Describing what makes it a special friendship.

- Subject: Henry
  Focus: Showing his abilities as a make-believe ballplayer.

- Subject: Samantha
  Focus: Describing situations that embarrass her.

- Subject: Rosie
  Focus: Showing how she is a daredevil.

- Subject: Mr. Crown
  Focus: Describing behaviors that make him seem grouchy and impatient.

- Subject: Lucas
  Focus: Showing why he is called a class clown.

- Subject: Karen
  Focus: Describing how she is a whiz.

As you begin to think about the character description you will be writing, you have already identified the subjects of your paragraphs by choosing characters from your novels, but what will the foci be? Think about the description of Jonathan: The subject was Jonathan, but what was the focus of the writer? (Give students time to develop a focus description; answers you might expect are that Jonathan had a very expressive face and you could really get to know him just watching his face, or Jonathan's face revealed his feelings and how he handled situations, or Jonathan's face told you what he was thinking and feeling.) Think again about the description of Ramona: The subject was Ramona, but what was the focus of the sketch? (Ramona felt tall, grown-up, and wise in the ways of the world.)

Review your prewrite brainstorming sheets and develop topic sentences for your character description sketches. Collaborate with your partners to discuss and refine the sentences.

Descriptive Paragraph

Topic Sentence

It has two parts: the subject and the focus. In the subject you identify the who or what of the paragraph and in the focus you share a feeling, an attitude, or a perspective about the subject.

Here are some examples:

1. Melissa didn't mind being a latch-key kid; in fact she felt pretty confident about her abilities to manage coming home alone.

2. Marcus was really shy and hated situations where he was the center of attention.

3. Grandma loves adventure!

4. Jeff and Megan share a magical friendship.

5. Henry is an amazing make-believe ballplayer.

6. Samantha embarrasses easily.

7. Rosie's nickname is "Daredevil."

8. Mr. Crown always seemed grouchy and impatient.

9. Lucas likes his role as class clown.

10. Karen is a whiz at everything she does.

➤ Figure 4.5. Topic Sentences

2. *Supporting detail sentences* explain and describe the topic and help the reader understand the focus of the writer. Look at the sketch about Ramona (see figure 4.4); can you identify the supporting detail sentences? How do they elaborate on the topic sentence?

    Why, what, and *how* questions are good strategies for building details. What kinds of questions would you ask yourself to help add details for the topic sentences? (Display the transparency of figure 4.6, but cover everything except the name of the first character; slowly reveal the questions after students have had an opportunity to suggest what they would ask themselves. Continue the process until you are sure students feel comfortable with the strategy.)

    Think about your topic sentences, then review the prewrite brainstorming sheets and circle words and phrases that add details in support of your description purposes. Use the circled information to continue writing the first drafts of your character sketches.

3. The *closing sentence* is the end of the paragraph and reminds the reader about the topic and the focus. Review the closing sentences in the Ramona sketch (see figure 4.4); how do they remind you of the focus of the paragraph? (Use the transparency of closing sentences [see figure 4.7] to show and discuss some other examples.) Add closing sentences to your character descriptions.

4. *Revising.* Conference about your sketches, thinking about the following questions:

    •   What details build understanding and acceptance of the topic focus?

    •   What part of the sketch seems unclear?

    •   How could you add details from the prewrite brainstorming?

5. *Editing.* Now edit your sketches for spelling, punctuation, and capitalization errors. An effective way to check for errors is to read your sketches from the bottom to the top; this reversal of order forces you to really look at each word and each line. Circle errors or use highlighting markers to indicate misspellings and punctuation and capitalization errors. Consult dictionaries to correct words and conference with peers to correct punctuation and capitalization errors.

6. *Publishing.* Draft and share final copies of your sketches.

Text continues on page 65.

Descriptive Paragraph

Supporting Detail Sentences

These sentences add information that explains and describes the topic and helps the reader understand the focus. Why, what, and how questions are good strategies for building details. Here are some question examples:

1. Melissa
What are her abilities? What are examples of her self-confidence?

2. Marcus
How does Marcus show that he is shy?   What happens to his face and body when he is the center of attention?

3. Grandma
What does Grandma do that shows she loves adventure?

4. Jeff and Megan
What are examples that show how special the friendship is?

5. Henry
Why is Henry amazing? What are his accomplishments?

6. Samantha
How does her face show embarrassment?

7. Rosie
What behaviors or adventures show that she is a daredevil?

8. Mr. Crown
What are examples of his grouchiness and impatience?

9. Lucas
How do we know that Lucas likes his role as a class clown? What thoughts and conversations show his enjoyment of this role?

10. Karen
What are her accomplishments? How quickly did she achieve these abilities?

➤ Figure 4.6. Supporting Detail Questions

Descriptive Paragraph

Closing Sentence

This sentence is the end of the paragraph and reminds the reader about the topic and the focus.

Here are some examples:

1. Melissa didn't mind being a latch-key kid; in fact she felt pretty confident about her abilities to manage coming home alone.
Closing: "Mom, don't worry. I can handle coming home alone after school."

2. Marcus was really shy and hated situations where he was the center of attention.
Closing: Marcus was determined never to be famous!

3. Grandma loves adventure!
Closing: As you can see, Grandma really loves excitement and the unexpected!

4. Jeff and Megan share a magical friendship.
Closing: Jeff and Megan will be friends forever.

5. Henry is an amazing make-believe ballplayer.
Closing: Henry thought to himself, "If only I could use my make-believe abilities in a real baseball game!"

6. Samantha embarrasses easily.
Closing: Samantha wished her face would not get red so easily.

7. Rosie's nickname is "Daredevil."
Closing: Rosie's reputation as a daredevil is well-earned.

➤ Figure 4.7. Closing Sentences

Descriptive Paragraph

ClosingSentence

8. Mr. Crown always seemed grouchy and impatient.
Closing: If you need help, don't let Mr. Crown's grouchy reaction stop you.

9. Lucas likes his role as class clown.
Closing: Lucas has a difficult time imagining a role where he isn't the class clown.

10. Karen is a whiz at everything she does.
Closing: Everything always comes easily to Karen.

➤ Figure 4.7. Closing Sentences (*cont.*)

➤ Activity Plan 6: Creating Your Own Characters

Materials

Writing journals
Transparency and multiple copies of the character pie (see activity sheet 4.3)

Engage

Write these words on the board, "If I were a writer . . . " Pause and let students think of responses to that starter, then list the students' ideas on the board. Their responses are an effective assessment of their level of understanding of the way writers work.

Elaborate

Address the students as follows:

Many writers create characters first, even before they have a story in mind. Character ideas can come from many places: friends and people you know, someone whom you admire, or even animals you have observed. Let's brainstorm a list of possibilities for characters. (If students are stumped, ideas that might spark other character suggestions are a boy who loves insects, a girl who collects baseball cards, a stray cat, a friend who is very tall for his or her age, a grandparent who is a champion fisher, a favorite hamster, a young sibling, a student who loves to draw, a relative who raises sheep, a friend who is a runner.)

Explore

Use one of the suggestions from the list and the transparency of the character pie (activity sheet 4.3) to model collecting details that describe the character: name, appearance, clothing, movements, personality traits, job or hobby or skill, and/or family background. (See figure 4.8 for an example.)

Have students record the character ideas (from their initial brainstorming) in their journals, then select one of the characters and complete a character pie (using activity sheet 4.3) about that character. Remind them that the largest section of the pie should describe what is most important to that character and encourage them to collaborate with peers to discuss and brainstorm descriptive ideas. Circulate as students work; use these questions to enhance students' thinking: What does the character's face tell us about his or her personality? What does the character most enjoy doing? When you imagine yourself inside this character's shoes, what thoughts do you hear going on inside the character's head? What makes you care about this character?

As students are completing their character pies, ask them to review what they have written and imagine a story that could develop from this information. (Remind students to keep the character pies in their writing journals.) (*Verbal/Linguistic Intelligence*)

Text continues on page 68.

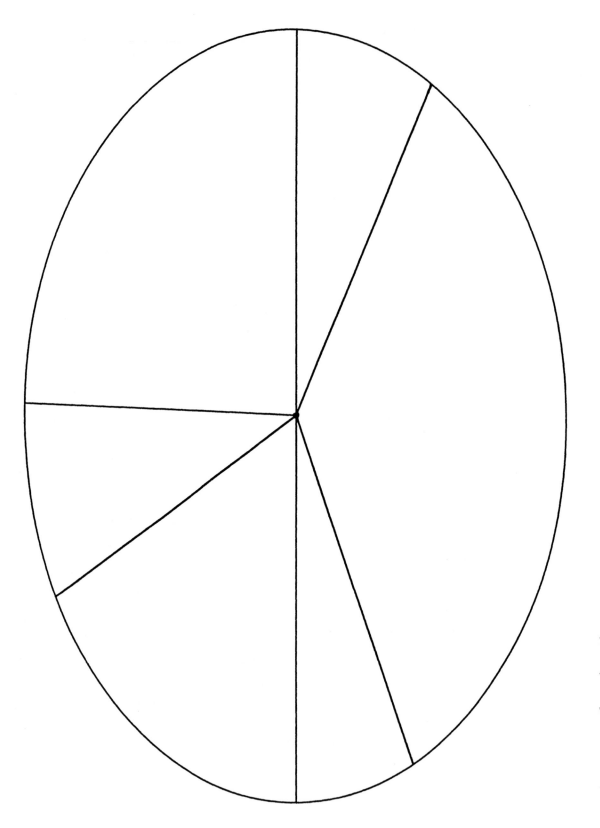

▶ Activity Sheet 4.3. Character Pie

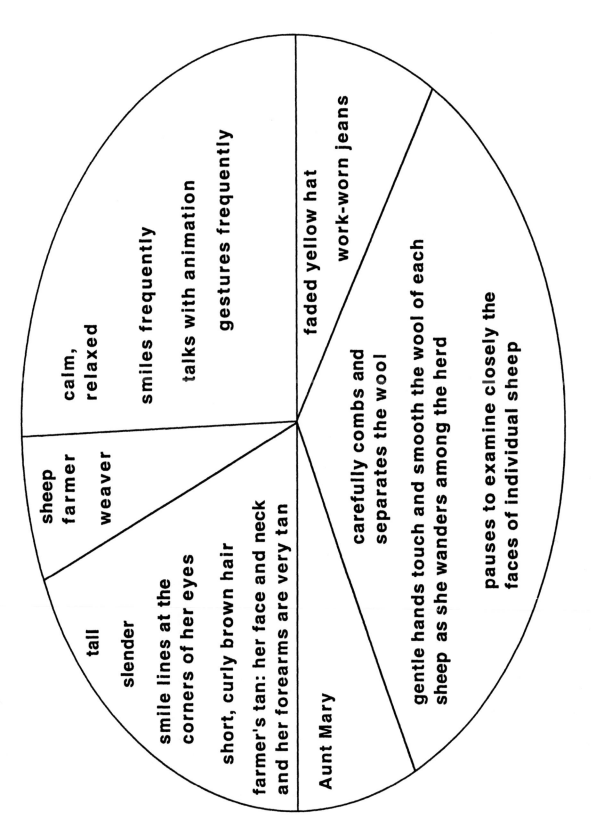

sheep
farmer
weaver

calm,
relaxed

smiles frequently

talks with animation

gestures frequently

tall

slender

smile lines at the
corners of her eyes

short, curly brown hair

farmer's tan: her face and neck
and her forearms are very tan

faded yellow hat

work-worn jeans

carefully combs and
separates the wool

gentle hands touch and smooth the wool of each
sheep as she wanders among the herd

pauses to examine closely the
faces of individual sheep

Aunt Mary

▶ Figure 4.8. Character Pie: Details About Aunt Mary

Connect

Invite students to share descriptive information from the pies and the story ideas they imagine from the character descriptions. (Repeat this process with the character pies until students have a wide variety of characters and story ideas in their writing journals. Invite them to select one idea and develop it into a story.)

➤Activity Plan 7: Writing the Story

Materials

Transparency of a completed character pie developed during the previous lesson (Use a character pie developed by a student or the one developed in the whole class modeling session.)

Transparency of activity sheet 4.4, Story Idea Web

Writing journals

Trip to the media center

Large sheet of butcher paper (Create a four-column chart in preparation for categorizing different kinds of leads in stories; see figure 4.9.)

Mirette on the High Wire by Emily Arnold McCully

Story Leads			
Questions?	Conversation (Dialogue)	Description	Other

➤Figure 4.9. Story Leads Chart

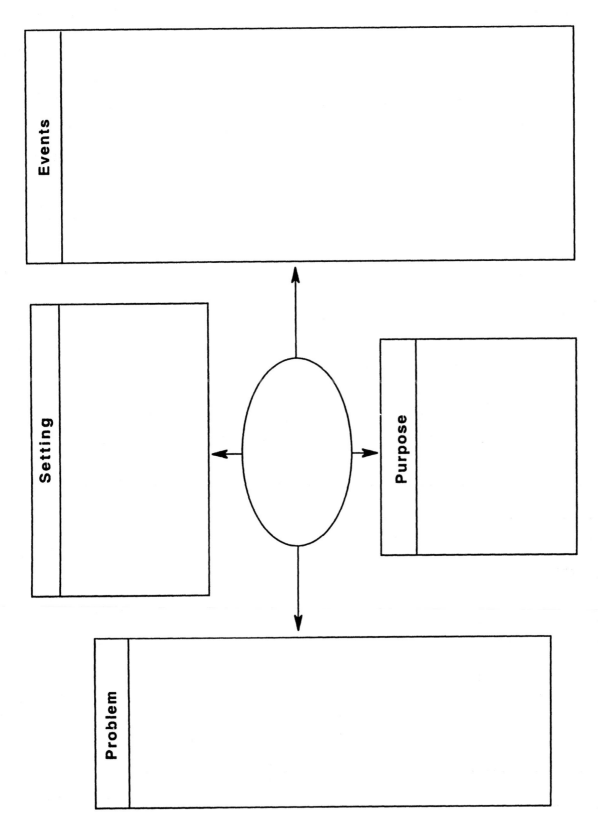

Events

Setting

Purpose

Problem

▶ Activity Sheet 4.4. Story Idea Web

Engage

For a prewriting activity, display a completed character pie and ask students to imagine story ideas from this character description. Select one idea to develop. (See figure 4.10 for an example of a story idea developed from the character pie about Aunt Mary.)

Elaborate

Use the transparency of the Story Idea Web (see activity sheet 4.4) to model how to plan a story. Describe what you are doing as you complete the web:

1.   The center circle lists the main character. Who is the main character of the story?

2.   The setting box describes where the story takes place. What words would you suggest to describe the setting?

3.   The problem box identifies the problem the main character needs to solve. What is the problem faced by the main character?

4.   The purpose box describes the mood or feeling of the story; the feeling or mood helps you choose the right words to make the story serious or suspenseful or funny. Will this story be serious, suspenseful, humorous, surprising, scary, or sad?

5.   The events box describes the sequence of the plot: rising action, climax, falling action. What are the events of the story? Refocus questions: What happens first? second? third? last? Which of these events is the climax of the story? (*Verbal/Linguistic Intelligence*)

Explore

Have students select characters from their character pie descriptions, then use the Story Idea Web (see activity sheet 4.4) to plan the development of their stories.

Once story ideas are planned, move to the media center and give students time to browse novels and picture books for leads to stories. Have them record at least three examples in their writing journals, then gather students in a circle and categorize their lead examples into the four columns listed on the butcher paper (see figure 4.9). Ask each student to share one example and list it in the appropriate column. Examples are:

1.   What ever happened to the good old days? (question)

2.   "Stay out of my room!" yelled Justin, as he slammed the door. (conversation)

3.   In the days when farmers worked with ox and plow, there lived a girl who loved to dream. (description)

4.   You wouldn't believe it, but I was born under the feed bin in the barn. (other: main character introduction)

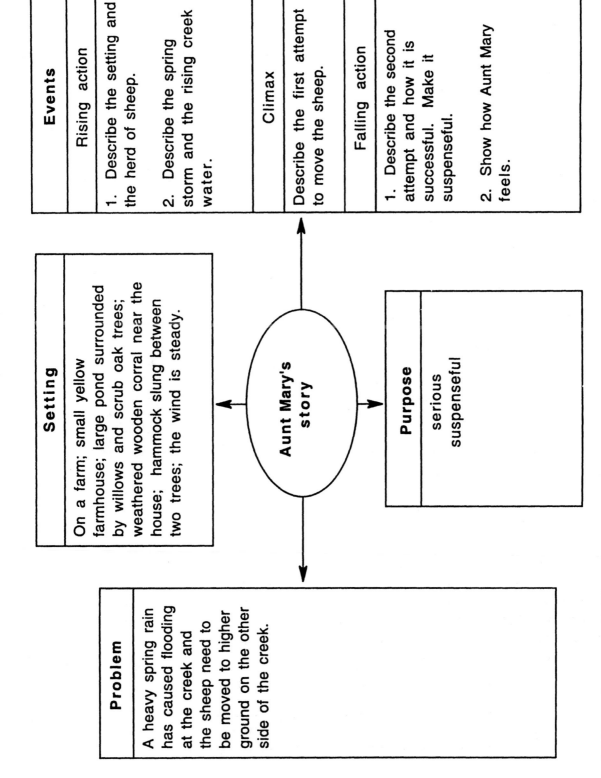

Setting

On a farm; small yellow farmhouse; large pond surrounded by willows and scrub oak trees; weathered wooden corral near the house; hammock slung between two trees; the wind is steady.

Events

Rising action

1. Describe the setting and the herd of sheep.

2. Describe the spring storm and the rising creek water.

Climax

Describe the first attempt to move the sheep.

Falling action

1. Describe the second attempt and how it is successful. Make it suspenseful.

2. Show how Aunt Mary feels.

Aunt Mary's story

Purpose

serious
suspenseful

Problem

A heavy spring rain has caused flooding at the creek and the sheep need to be moved to higher ground on the other side of the creek.

▶ Figure 4.10. Aunt Mary's Story

Return to the classroom and have students complete the rough drafting stage of their writing. Display the lead examples and encourage students to develop leads for their stories, then continue writing rough drafts, using the character pies and the story web planning sheets. (*Verbal/ Linguistic Intelligence*)

Connect

Have students revise their writing, focusing on sequence, details, and dialogue.

Sequence

Have students exchange their stories with partners. One partner should read aloud the story written by the other partner. This process of sharing will help the writer recognize what is unclear or missing in the story and he or she can work on clarity and reorganization. (*Interpersonal Intelligence*)

Details

Have students circle or highlight the nouns in their stories, then check to see what descriptive details they have used; for example, if a sentence read, "Aunt Mary lived on a farm in southern Iowa," the student would have circled *Aunt Mary*, *farm*, and *Iowa*. Revision for details might change the sentence to read, "Aunt Mary lived on a small, well-kept farm in the gently rolling hills of southern Iowa." Have students challenge themselves to add details to at least one noun in each sentence. (*Verbal/Linguistic Intelligence*)

Dialogue

Use various pages in *Mirette on the High Wire* to model revising for dialogue. Share the first example below by reading the text as it is written in the story, then reading the suggested change. Share the second example by reading the text as it is written, but ask for students' suggestions for making it into dialogue. After a short discussion, share the suggested dialogue below. Repeat this process with the third example below.

1. On the third page, the second sentence of narration could be changed to dialogue: "I am Bellini, a retired high-wire walker," the stranger explained.

2. On the fourth page, Mirette's thoughts could be changed to dialogue: "Of all the things a person can do, this must be the most magical. My feet tingle as if they want to jump up on the wire beside Bellini," Mirette exclaimed.

3. On page 19, Bellini's thoughts could also be changed to dialogue: "I feel terrible disappointing Mirette. If I don't face my fear, I can't face Mirette. I must try to walk the wire," Bellini stated with determination.

Write an example on the board so that students see how to use quotation marks, ending punctuation, and correct capitalization. Have students return to their stories and read and mark them for places for dialogue; they can add dialogue or revise narration so it reads like dialogue. (*Verbal/ Linguistic Intelligence*)

Editing

Have students check for spelling, punctuation, and capitalization errors and make corrections.

Publishing

Have students draft final versions of their stories; remind them about indentation of paragraphs and for dialogue. Have students plan and complete watercolor illustrations to accompany the stories. (*Verbal/Linguistic and Visual/Spatial Intelligences*)

5 Owl Moon

Written by Jane Yolen
Illustrated by John Schoenherr
New York: Philomel Books, 1987

Summary

➤ Late one winter night a little girl and her father go owling. Their feet crunch over the crisp snow as they trek silently into the forest to a clearing in the woods, where Pa makes his call to the owl. Soon after, an answering call echoes through the trees and Pa catches the owl in the light of his flashlight just as it lands on a branch in the clearing. Silently they stare at one another, then the great owl pumps its wings and lifts off into the night sky. Pa and the little girl joyfully return home.

Award Year

➤ 1988

Art Information

➤ Illustrated using watercolors and pen and ink.

Curriculum Connections

➤ Descriptive writing, observation, birds

➤Activity Plan 1: Sharing the Story

Materials

Two small signs listing these topic sentences: "Silence is important." and "This is a special outing." (see figure 5.1).
Drawing paper
Paintbrushes and watercolors
Caldecott Award poster
Pen and ink (available at art supply stores, or use a fine point black marker)

Silence is important.	**This is a special outing.**

➤Figure 5.1. *Owl Moon* Signs

Engage

Set the stage for sharing the story: Dim the lights, gather the students in a semicircle in front of you, lean forward, and whisper, "Shhhhh!, listen, can you hear it?" Pause expectantly, and then quietly hoot like an owl several times. (*Bodily/Kinesthetic Intelligence*)

Elaborate

Introduce the story and ask students to carefully notice how Yolen lets us know that silence is important. Pause and display the silence sign. Ask the students how they know this is a special outing. Pause and show the special outing sign. Share the story.

Explore

Ask the students: What words and phrases give you the feelings of that night walk? What phrases do you particularly like? How do you know it's a cold night? How does Yolen show the silence of that night? (Record and save students' responses.)

Connect

Have students draw and paint favorite scenes from the book.

Share the Caldecott Award information:

1. As students examine the cover of the book, ask them what special thing they notice. (gold medal) Ask them what the name of the medal is. (Caldecott Award Medal) Ask them why it has been placed on this book. (Some answers may be: The illustrations are special, well done, particularly interesting, exciting, and/or unusual.)

2. Discuss the art techniques used in creating the pictures:

   > We've talked about how the words and phrases of the story give us the feelings of the night walk. How do the illustrations add to the mood of the night walk? [Browse the illustrations, taking particular notice of the bare-limbed trees, the shadows, the sense of space in several of the illustrations contrasted with the closed, encircled feeling of the dark woods, and miles of the never-ending snow.]

   > Watercolors and pen and ink are the media used in this book. You can really see how necessary and effective the pen-and-ink detail is in the illustrations. [Browse again.] The watercolors seem to add a layer of translucence and help us feel the cold of the night.

3. Ask two student volunteers to search the poster for the year the story won. (Searching the poster helps students become familiar with the many different titles selected for the award.)

➤ Activity Plan 2: Working As a Writer— Noticing Details

Materials

Oranges, enough so each child receives a small slice to eat

Knife

Cutting board

Two to three outdoor settings (Select settings that provide opportunities for thorough observations and descriptions: a nature setting, a cityscape, a museum, a library, the zoo, a portion of the playground.)

Writing journals (Writing journals are notebooks that students carry with them constantly to record ideas such as responses to and descriptions of things they see and experience, interesting words, flashes of imagination, "what if" speculations, and connections sparked by books, speakers, and films; writing journals can also hold meaningful photographs, lists, sketches, newspaper clippings, ticket stubs, and other memorabilia, anything that provides seeds for writing. Spiral notebooks work well; encourage students to use these journals exclusively for writing and to resist tearing pages from the journals for other assignments.)

Engage

Write this phrase on the board: "Show don't tell: sights, sounds, smells, feelings." Invite students to discuss the meaning of the words and why they are important for a writer. Discuss how Ms. Yolen shows that silence is important: The little girl never calls out, she stops and waits patiently in the clearing, she shrugs rather than talking when there isn't an immediate response to the owl call, they walk on but they never say a word, and she doesn't ask questions when they enter the woods, even though she wonders about what is hiding in the dark beyond the trees. All of these words and phrases convey the importance of quiet in the owling journey.

Following are examples of writing that show rather than tell. Ask the students: In the first description about the dog, what details make the reader know that Scruffy was a mischief maker but was still loved? As you share the second description, pause before reading the last sentence and ask students to identify the feeling that has been described. (embarrassment) Then read the last sentence.

Scruffy

Scruffy is a lovable mischief maker. He steals the socks I leave on the bedroom floor and sneaks them under the bed. He can't resist wastebaskets and frequently I find trails of trash throughout the house. All of the floor plants are wrapped in brown towels because he loves to dig in the dirt surrounding the plants. His favorite command is "fetch" because he knows it will be a wonderful game of tag . . . me chasing him to grab the newspaper or the shoe and he running in wild circles. Because of Scruffy, we don't use tablecloths on the kitchen table anymore; he grabbed the corner of the cloth and tugged and pulled until everything came tumbling to the floor. It wasn't that he was really hungry; he just likes our food as a treat. When I scold him, he just looks at me with one ear cocked in puzzlement, his tail thumping the floor, then he leaps to lick my face in greeting and happiness and I can't help hugging him and giving him a kiss in return.

It Couldn't Happen Again!

I looked down and couldn't believe my eyes; somehow in my hurry to get to the school bus stop on time, I'd left the house dressed in my Mickey Mouse slippers. I looked hurriedly around to see if any of my friends had arrived and saw Emily staring at my feet. This would never happen to Emily; she was always perfectly organized and perfectly dressed. I wanted to sink through the sidewalk and disappear. This was the worst day of my life. I tried to hide one foot behind the other, but it was no use; there was no way to hide the slippers. Surely, there was time to run back home and change; oh no, the bus was coming around the corner and if I missed the bus I wouldn't get to school. I held my head high as I stepped into the bus, but the titters and sly looks began as soon as the kids spotted my feet. I could feel my neck turning red, then my face as I slinked to the back of the bus and hid in the last seat. When we stopped for Susan and she saw my feet and asked what happened, I couldn't even explain, I was feeling so low! How would I ever get through the day? This had to be my most embarrassing moment.

Elaborate

Use the following activities to further emphasize and practice the "showing not telling" writing technique.

Ask the students how they would show their happiness and pleasure when a wish comes true. Use wait time to give students time to plan responses, then write this topic sentence: "My Wish Came True." Have students mime their responses and, as they demonstrate, record under the topic sentence words and phrases describing what the audience sees. Some responses may be jumping up and down in excitement, running into a room to share the wish with a friend or relative, a huge grin, a contented sigh, and/or counting the days on a calendar between making the wish and its fulfillment. (*Bodily/Kinesthetic Intelligence*)

Slice the oranges and give each student a slice. Ask them how they would show enjoyment in eating the orange. Don't forget wait time (let students eat the orange slices and think about their charade dramatizations), then use this topic sentence, "The Orange Was the Best I Had Ever Eaten." Again, record words and phrases as they demonstrate their hunger and enjoyment. The students' responses may include eating the orange slice hurriedly, smelling the orange before slicing it, making enjoyment noises, slurping the juice before eating the slice, licking fingers, and/or looking around for more. (*Bodily/Kinesthetic Intelligence*)

Explore

Address the children as follows:

As we discovered, Jane Yolen, the author of *Owl Moon*, is a writer who is especially good at showing and not telling writing. What were some of the "showing" words and phrases we identified? [the brightness of the moon making the sky shine like day; the words that let the reader know that this is a special outing; after the girl's usual bedtime, her statement that she had been waiting a long time for this outing; her comments about her brothers; the imagery she uses in describing the clearing in the dark woods; listening and looking "so hard"; the feeling of hope fulfilled when the owl lands on the branch and is captured by Pa's flashlight]

Travel to the outdoor setting and have students sit or stand, quietly absorbing the sights and sounds before beginning to write. Encourage students to focus on one aspect of the setting (a person, an object, an event, a sound, a part of the setting like the sky or the ground, a building or a tree, etc.). Ask the students what sights, sounds, smells, and physical feelings are evoked by what they are describing. Invite students to share their observations; continue writing and sharing until restlessness develops.

Connect

Over the next few days, repeat this process with other settings and continue to invite students to share their writing. (*Visual/Spatial and Verbal/Linguistic Intelligences*)

➤ Activity Plan 3: Working As a Writer—Using Similes

Engage

Have students draw small rectangles (three or four inches by two or three inches) on their papers and respond to the following poem by drawing what they see:

> billowing clouds,
> white sails,
> crowding in the south.

Have students share their pictures and discuss how in the poet's eye the two different images are alike (the clouds and the sails seem indistinguishable; their shapes seem to blend as one). Refocus question: What are the two objects the poet compares? How are they similar? How does the comparison help in drawing the pictures?

Make a new rectangle and share the following poem. Have students draw again:

in the moonlight,
the white plum tree
becomes again
a tree of winter.

Share the drawings and discuss the comparisons. Ask the students: Why does the poet make the connection between the white-blossomed plum tree and a wintertime tree? How are the two trees similar? (The plum tree is a mass of blossoms and in the white brightness of the moonlight, it looks as though its branches are covered in snow.) How does this comparison help the listener really see the images the poet describes?

Elaborate

Address the students as follows:

These comparisons help readers understand and imagine the images described by the writer. There are two ways to write these types of comparisons. A simile uses the words *like* or *as* in describing the comparison; for example, "clean as a whistle," "silent as a snake," "mad as a hornet," or "laughing like a hyena." A metaphor doesn't use *like* or *as*, it just makes a statement; for example, "I was a shadow as I walked home," or "Stars are diamonds that light up the sky."

Have students search *Owl Moon* and list and discuss the similes and metaphors they find. Ask them: How do the comparisons of trees as statues and the train whistle and a sad song build powerful images? What is the quiet of a dream? How does the light of a winter moon make a silver mask? How does the comparison of the color of the snow with the familiar experience of milk in a cereal bowl build a stronger understanding? What is a shadow without sound?

Explore

Have students return to their journals to review their outdoor setting observations and look for opportunities to add similes.

Connect

Have students share similes they have written and discuss their excitement about making their observations come alive with powerful imagery.

➤Activity Plan 4: What Makes a Bird a Bird?

Materials

Bird sounds tapes (Northsound Music produces two tapes—one on yard, garden, and city birds and one on birds of the countryside; P.O. Box 1360, Minocqua, WI 54548, 800-726-6784; cost: $12.95 per tape. Houghton Mifflin also produces bird sound tapes on CD—one for birds of eastern and central North America [cost $20.00] and one for birds of western North America [cost $25.00]; P.O. Box 7050, Wilmington, MA 01887, 800-225-3362.)

Video about birds (Coronet produces a short video that shows a variety of birds, their adaptations to various habitats, and the characteristics they have in common; 2349 Chaffee Dr., St. Louis, MO 63146, 800-777-8100; cost: $59.00.)

Binoculars (several pairs)

Engage

Use the musical/rhythmic intelligence to introduce the daily bird activities and capture the students' attention with birdsongs. After listening to the songs, have the students try to identify the birds.

Elaborate

Begin a web listing characteristics of birds (see figure 5.2).

Explore

Watch the video and add information to the web. (*Visual/Spatial and Verbal/Linguistic Intelligences*)

Connect

Go on a bird-watching expedition. Take binoculars and writing journals for drawing and describing the birds students see. (*Naturalist, Visual/Spatial, and Verbal/Linguistic Intelligences*)

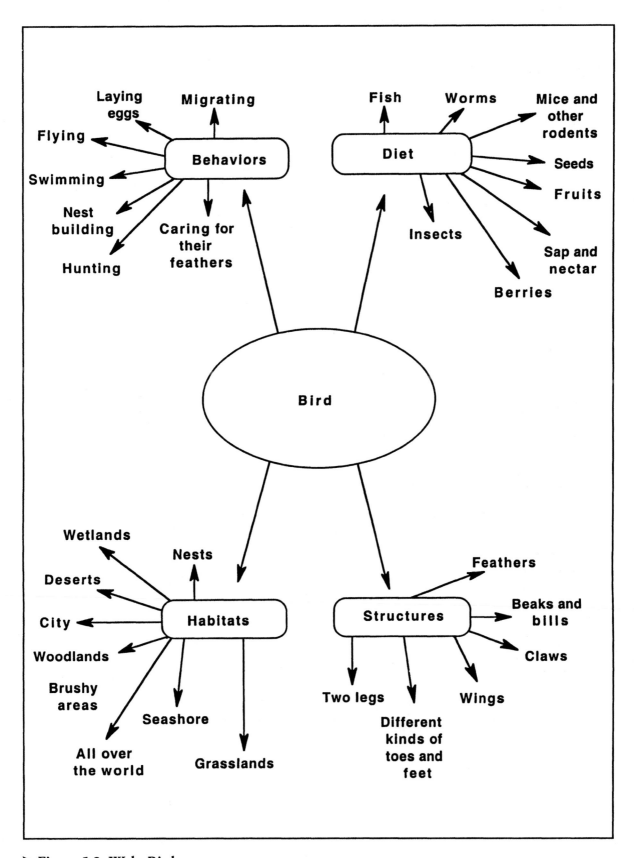

►Figure 5.2. Web: Birds

➤ Activity Plan 5: Who Lives There?

Materials

Bird sounds tape used in Activity Plan 4
Shoe boxes (one per partnership/group)
Materials for habitats (construction paper; wallpaper; glue; scissors; natural materials such as twigs, grass, sand, pinecones)

Engage

Play the bird sounds and see if students can identify the birds making the songs.

Elaborate

Begin discussion and instruction on where birds live. Have students think about the bird-watching expedition and *Owl Moon*, and discuss different kinds of habitats: forest, brushy area, meadow, marsh, city park, farm, suburban yard, tropical rain forest, desert, Arctic tundra, ocean, and sandy beach. Ask students to identify some characteristics of each. (See figure 5.3.)

Explore

Have students work in pairs or small groups to select habitats, research, and create three-dimensional habitat miniatures using shoe boxes. They should add birds to the habitats and investigate the adaptations birds have made that help them survive in the habitats. For example, the roadrunner makes its nest in a cactus because the sharp spines of the plant keep away predators. Its dark skin absorbs the sun's warming rays to help it through the cold nights, its sharp beak helps spear and stab prey like rattlesnakes, and its speedy legs help it run smoothly over the sand. (*Interpersonal and Bodily/Kinesthetic Intelligences*)

Connect

Have students present their habitat displays and explain to the class the structures and behaviors of their birds that allow them to survive in their habitats.

Habitats	Characteristics	Birds	Adaptations
Forest	Dense growth of trees	Warblers, Orioles, Creepers, Nuthatches	Expert climbers
Open woodland	Scattered trees	Waxwings, Woodpeckers, Wrens, Grosbeaks, Flickers	Expert climbers
Meadow	Tall prairie grasses	Kestrels, Cowbirds, Meadow larks	Three-toed for scratching & digging
Brushy areas	Bushes, low scrubby trees	Catbirds, Shrikes, Towhees	Color camouflage
Desert	Cacti, sand, plateaus	Quails, Roadrunners, Eagles, Owls	Low water needs, night hunters
Marsh	Cattails, lily pads, near lakes, ponds or rivers	Loons, Grebes, Rails, Ducks, Herons	Webbed feet, fish and water plant eaters
Coastal	Beach grasses, near oceans	Gulls, Terns, Plovers, Pelicans	Webbed feet, fish and seaweed eaters
Rainforest	Dense growth of trees	Toucan, Ibis, Parrot, Quetzel	Color camouflage
City	Trees, shrubs, buildings, birdhouses	Robins, Jays, Sparrows, Cardinals	Nest in many places
Arctic	Snow, ice, almost treeless marshland	Plovers, Terns, Ptarmigans	Camouflage, migration

▶ Figure 5.3. Bird Habitats

➤Activity Plan 6: The Work of Feathers

Materials

Selection of bird feathers (Available at hobby and craft stores; can be ordered from Delta Education, P.O. Box 915, Hudson, NH 03051, 800-258-1302, or from Nasco, 901 Janesville Ave., Fort Atkinson, WI, 800-558-9595; cost: about $1.00 per package of five.)

Engage

Write the word *feathers* and list the four kinds of feathers: *down, wing, tail,* and *body.* Distribute feathers and let students explore their flight possibilities and speculate on the kinds of feathers they are investigating. (*Bodily/Kinesthetic Intelligence*)

Elaborate

Explain to the students that wing feathers are the flight tools for the bird; the outer and inner wing feathers have irregular shape and design and provide power, stability, and steering during flight. Down feathers lie close to the bird's skin and keep birds warm and insulated from the weather. Some body feathers have developed for display and others are used to insulate and cover the bird; tail feathers are used for steering, balancing, and courtship. Have students find and share other information about feathers.

Explore

Feather care movements include preening (cleaning), molting (shedding), oiling (part of preening), dusting (bathing in dust instead of water), and anting (letting ants crawl over the body to kill mites and other parasites). Invite student participation and demonstrate flight movements, including soaring, gliding, upstroke, and downstroke. (*Bodily/Kinesthetic Intelligence*)

Connect

Discuss why male birds are often brightly colored and the females rather dull in color. Have students imagine themselves as birds and write paragraphs describing soaring like a bird.

➤ Activity Plan 7: Eat Like a Bird

Materials

Scale
Bird feeder supplies (millet, sunflower seeds, cracked corn, other types of seeds, raisins, bits of apples or bananas, peanuts, peanut butter suet)
Materials to build two bird feeder trays

Engage

Display a scale in front of the class and drop small items into it while you pose the questions: Have you ever heard the expression "to eat like a bird"? What does this mean?

Tell students that birds burn up a lot of energy and many birds eat twice their weight in food each day. Ask them how many pounds of food we would have to eat in a day "to eat like birds." Brainstorm a typical menu for the day and estimate how much each item weighs; for example, a bowl of cereal would equal four ounces, a glass of milk, eight ounces, a glass of juice, eight ounces. Estimate the average weight of students at the grade level involved in the bird unit and double that weight. How much food would this student have to eat to "eat like a bird"? Review the menu and increase the quantities so they eventually weigh double the weight of the student. For example, how many bowls of cereal would the student eat? (Four bowls would equal a pound.) How many glasses of milk and juice? (Eight glasses would be four pounds.) (*Logical/Mathematical Intelligence*)

Elaborate

Brainstorm a list of what birds eat. If necessary, do some research on bird-feeding habits to draw a variety of species of birds to the feeders. (*Verbal/Linguistic Intelligence*)

Explore

Construct and fill the bird feeders. (*Bodily/Kinesthetic Intelligence*)

Connect

Conduct experiments to chart information about the use of the feeders. Have the students write expository paragraphs (paragraphs giving information about topics) using the information that has been charted during the experiments.

Experiment 1

Ask the students: What time of day are the feeders busiest? Is there a pattern to their use?

Experiment 2

Use the bird feeders to determine seed popularity. Put different seeds and foods in the feeders and have the students record which birds eat which foods. They should determine which food is most popular. (*Bodily/Kinesthetic, Verbal/Linguistic, and Logical/Mathematical Intelligences*)

➤ Activity Plan 8: Exploring a Food Chain

Materials

Material for marking a large circle on the playground (baseball chalk, spray paint, rope, or hose)
Cottontails (made from cotton balls glued to construction paper circles)
Coyote tails (made from brown construction paper)
Pieces of yellow yarn (clover in bloom)
Masking tape
Food chain materials: index cards (at least twelve per student partnership), hole punch (one per partnership), yarn, scissors (one per partnership), pencils

Engage

Divide the class into three groups (rabbits, coyotes, and clover) and tell the students that this role play takes place on the tall grass prairie. Have the rabbits tape the cottontails to their lower back clothing, the coyotes tape their tails to lower back clothing, and the clovers hold small pieces of yellow yarn. The rabbits should crouch in the middle of a large open area, ready to hop for nibbles of sweet clover. The coyotes should surround the rabbits. (Have the students form a large circle with outstretched arms and fingertips touching the neighboring coyotes. Mark this circle and remind the coyotes that they must stay inside this circle.) The clovers should spread out in a larger circle surrounding the coyotes, five to ten feet away. The clovers may not move.

Rabbits eat clover and coyotes eat rabbits; for the rabbits to get the clovers, they must cross through coyote territory without losing their cottontails and take yarn from the clovers. The coyotes must grab rabbit tails to be fed (as rabbits pass through the circle). The clovers just wait to be eaten because they are plants and make their own food from sunlight energy. Once students lose their tails (get eaten) they must freeze. After a while, all the clover will be eaten and the rabbits will have no food; eventually the coyotes will also be out of food.

Ask the students: How does this experience represent a food chain? (Clovers are plants and use sunlight to make energy, rabbits are herbivores and eat the plants, coyotes are carnivores and eat the rabbits.) How would the food chain change if one of the organisms died out? What happens when there are too many coyotes and not enough rabbits? (*Bodily/Kinesthetic Intelligence*)

Elaborate

Write these vocabulary words on the board: *producer, consumer, predator, prey, carnivore, herbivore, omnivore, scavenger, decomposer*. Use the food chain simulation to define them. Make a flow chart showing their connections (see figure 5.4). Discuss with the students why predators are valuable in a community. (*Verbal/Linguistic and Logical/Mathematical Intelligences*)

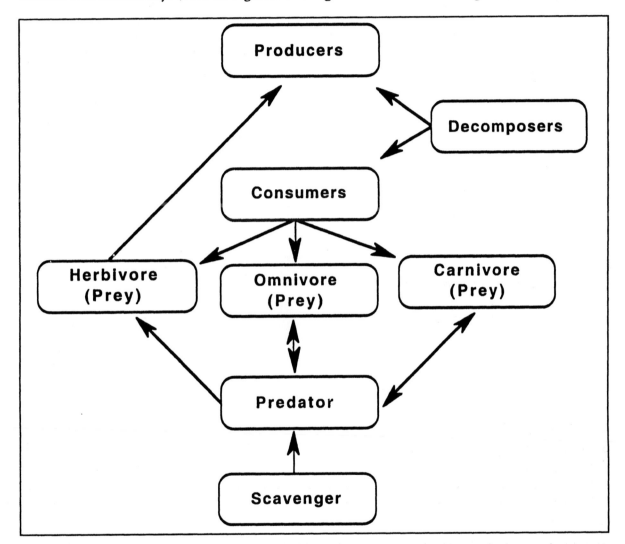

➤ **Figure 5.4. Flow Chart: Food Chain**

Hand out the food chain vocabulary sheet (activity sheet 5.1) and review the terms with the students.

Vocabulary	
Food Chain	This is the transfer of energy from the sun to producers, then to consumers
Producer	This is a living thing that makes its own food. Plants are producers; they use sunlight, water, and carbon dioxide to make food
Consumer	This is a living thing that cannot make its own food Animals cannot make their own food; they get food from other living things
Community	This is a group of producers and consumers
Predator	This is an animal that hunts and eats other animals
Carnivore	This is an animal that stalks/hunts for meat
Herbivore	This is an animal that gathers and grazes on plants
Omnivore	This is an animal that eats animals and plants
Scavenger	This is an animal that eats the remains of recently dead organisms
Decomposer	These are organisms that "break down" materials
Prey	These are animals eaten by predators

➤Activity Sheet 5.1. Food Chain Vocabulary

Explore

Have students work in partnerships using the food chain activity sheet (activity sheet 5.2) to discover the food chains they can make. (*Bodily/Kinesthetic and Logical/Mathematical Intelligences*)

Be sure each partnership has the necessary supplies (index cards, hole punch, yarn, and scissors) and starts by writing the names of the plants and animals on the index cards, one name per card. After punching holes in each end of the cards, students should join the cards to make food chains.

Connect

Share food chains and discuss how these were constructed. Ask the students: How many of the food chains included the boy? What generalizations can you make about the interdependence of life in a community?

Work with students to develop statements similar to these:

1. Plants are producers, and consumers like herbivores, carnivores, and omnivores eat producers.

2. A community includes producers and consumers like herbivores, carnivores, omnivores, scavengers, and decomposers.

3. If predators can't find prey, then they can eventually become endangered and the community changes.

➤ Activity Plan 9: Owl Pellets

Materials

Owl pellets (available from Delta Education, P.O. Box 3000, Nashua, NH 03061-3000; cost: $54.00, includes fifteen pellets, charts, and teacher's guide)

Engage

Look again at *Owl Moon* and relive the experience of owling. Have students practice calling to an owl as Pa did. (*Musical/Rhythmic and Visual/Spatial Intelligences*)

Elaborate

Have students investigate the diet of the owl and speculate on what they expect to see as they cut and sort the owl pellets. Write their predictions on the board. (*Verbal/Linguistic and Logical/Mathematical Intelligences*)

Food Chains

Names:

Task: What food chains can you make?	**Supplies:** index cards, hole punch, yarn, pencil

Steps:

1. Look at the list of plants and animals.

2. Write the name of the plant or animal on each card. Write only one name on each card.

3. Punch a hole in each end of the cards.

4. Use the yarn to join cards to make the food chains.

Challenges:

What is the longest food chain you can make?

What is the shortest food chain you can make?

How can you join one of your food chains with one from another group?

Choices:

Coyote	Hawk	Mouse
Deer	Caterpillar	Horse
Clover	Cat	Leaves
Boy	Robin	Sunflower seeds

►Activity Sheet 5.2. Food Chain Activity Sheet

Explore

Have students work in small groups to cut open owl pellets and identify the contents. Have them use the owl pellet activity sheet (activity sheet 5.3) to record information from their investigations. (*Logical/Mathematical Intelligence*)

Connect

Pose these questions for discussion: Why is the owl considered a predator? How is the owl adapted to its role as a nocturnal predator? What kinds of animals did the owl eat? What is the owl's community? (*Verbal/Linguistic Intelligence*)

➤ Activity Plan 10: A Nest Is My Home

Materials

Yarn and string (small lengths)

Engage

Display a variety of materials that might be found in nests (yarn, grasses, twigs, strings, rocks, mosses, mud, seed heads) and ask students what they might use if they were building a nest.

Elaborate

Take a trip outside and place short lengths of yarn and string (five to ten inches long) in grassy and brushy areas. Have students check each day and note what has been taken. (*Naturalist Intelligence*)

Explore

To build awareness about birds' nests, have students make a chart showing different kinds of birds' nests. Encourage them to consult and cooperate with each other so that many different kinds are shown. (*Logical/Mathematical and Naturalist Intelligences*)

Connect

Have students write a descriptive paragraph (paragraph that describes a person, a place, a thing, or an idea) about the kind of nest they would build. (*Verbal/Linguistic Intelligence*)

| Name_____ | Owl Pellet Investigation |

Owls are nocturnal (night-time) predators. In this activity you will examine owl pellets (undigested food coughed up by an owl) to identify the diet of an owl. **Safety Precaution:** Use the dissecting probes to cut open and carefully examine the contents. Do not use your hands.

| **Hypothesis:** If the owl is a night-time predator, what do you think will be the contents of the owl pellet? | **Procedure:**
1. Remove the aluminum foil from the owl pellet.
2. Cut open the pellet and spread out the remains of the owl's meal. **Remember the safety precaution.**
3. Separate the bones and try to identify parts of the prey's skeleton. |

Reporting: Describe your process of identification and your results. What conclusions can you make?

➤ Activity Sheet 5.3. Owl Pellets Investigation

➤ Activity Plan 11: Fact or Fable—What Do You Know?

Materials

Animal Fact/Animal Fable by Seymour Simon (New York: Crown, 1979)
Fact/Fable Statements (activity sheet 5.4; cut the statements into strips and place
 them in a basket or box)
Fact/Fable Page Forms (activity sheet 5.5; one per student)
Illustrating materials (crayons, markers, colored pencils)

Engage

Share Seymour Simon's book, *Animal Fact/Animal Fable.* (This book will form the basis
for a similar book on bird facts and fables, and each student will select one bird fact or fable statement
and contribute a page.) (*Visual/Spatial and Verbal/Linguistic Intelligences*)

Elaborate

Have students draw their assignments from the fact/fable statements in the basket (see
activity sheet 5.4). Before students conduct any research, have them respond to the fact/fable statements and draw humorous pictures. Paste these on individual fact/fable pages (see activity sheet 5.5)
and have students write their statements in the lower part of the pages (see figure 5.5).

Explore

Begin research so students can discover whether the statements are facts or fables. Have
them explain their decisions by writing expository paragraphs, then revise their paragraphs using the
mini-lesson experiences for writing "well-developed" paragraphs (see lesson that follows).

Connect

After paragraphs have been revised and edited, have students publish final copies by
writing explanations on the reverse sides of their fact/fable pages. They should also create a second
more realistic illustration and add this to the explanation (see figure 5.5).

As a class, brainstorm a name for the book, create a cover, write an introduction, and
put the book together, then share the book.

Text continues on page 99.

Fact or Fable: Eagles have excellent eyesight.

Fact or Fable: Birds have several kinds of feathers.

Fact or Fable: Birds have bones like human beings.

Fact or Fable: "Like water off a duck's back" means birds are not bothered by anything.

Fact or Fable: Birds and reptiles molt.

Fact or Fable: Birds migrate because they do not like where they live.

Fact or Fable: If an animal has feathers, it must be a bird.

Fact or Fable: Penguins are birds.

Fact or Fable: The largest bird is the pelican.

Fact or Fable: Pelicans carry things in their beaks.

Fact or Fable: Birds build many kinds of nests.

➤ Activity Sheet 5.4. Fact/Fable Statements

Fact or Fable: Birds of prey eat live animals.

Fact or Fable: A grouse is a partridge.

Fact or Fable: The roadrunner, a desert bird, is a member of the cuckoo family.

Fact or Fable: Owls are wise old birds.

Fact or Fable: Baby geese will choose the first animal they see to be their Mom or Dad.

Fact or Fable: All birds fly.

Fact or Fable: All bird toes look alike.

Fact or Fable: Only birds have wings.

Fact or Fable: Birds have teeth.

Fact or Fable: The food a bird eats is determined by the kind of beak it has.

Fact or Fable: Hummingbirds fly like not other bird.

Fact or Fable: Birds hatch from eggs.

► Activity Sheet 5.4. Fact/Fable Statements (*cont.*)

Fact or Fable:

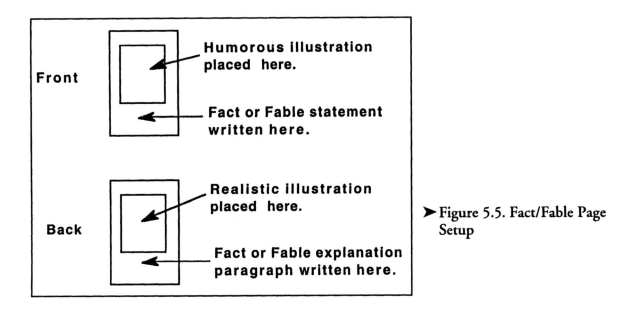

➤Figure 5.5. Fact/Fable Page Setup

Following is an example of an expository paragraph written for the fact/fable statement about bird nests:

> **Fact.** Birds do build many kinds of nests. Sometimes birds weave hanging nests, while other birds build their nests in the tall grass with weeds and grass. The whippoorwill makes dents in the leaves for her nest and robins build with sticks and mud. They line their nests with grass. A hummingbird builds its nest with soft plants and spider webs. It is no bigger than a marshmallow. A kingfisher builds in a hole in a mud bank. A tern sometimes lays eggs on a bare rock and the eggs look like little rocks. Bird nests come in all shapes and sizes.

Answers to the Fact or Fable Activity Sheet

Eagles have excellent eyesight. (fact)
Birds have several kinds of feathers. (fact)
Birds have bones like human beings. (fable)
"Like water off a duck's back" means birds are not bothered by anything. (fable)
Birds and reptiles molt. (fact)
Birds migrate because they do not like where they live. (fable)
If an animal has feathers, it must be a bird. (fact)
Penguins are birds. (fact)
The largest bird is the pelican. (fable)
Pelicans carry things in their beaks. (fable)
Birds build many kinds of nests. (fact)
Birds of prey eat live animals. (fact)
A grouse is a partridge. (fable)
The roadrunner, a desert bird, is a member of the cuckoo family. (fact)
Owls are wise old birds. (fable)
Baby geese will choose the first animal they see to be their mom or dad. (fact)
All birds fly. (fable)
All bird toes look alike. (fable)
Only birds have wings. (fable)
Birds have teeth. (fable)
The food a bird eats is determined by the kind of beak it has. (fact)
Hummingbirds fly like no other bird. (fact)
Birds hatch from eggs. (fact)

➤Activity Plan 12: Revising Paragraph Structure

Materials

Charlotte's Web by E. B. White (New York: Harper & Row, 1952)

Engage

Share the paragraph on page 42 of *Charlotte's Web*, which talks about early summer days on the farm.

Elaborate

Use the following questions and explanations to discuss the structure of the paragraph:

What is the focus of this paragraph? [The response should be: early summer days on a farm.] This becomes the topic of the paragraph. How is the focus sentence broad rather than narrow? [A variety of sentences can follow from this topic sentence.] How does the author elaborate and support this opening focus? [Responses should include phrases about the lilacs, the apple blossoms, the bees, the days, etc.] How does the author close the paragraph? [Students should share the last sentence.] The closing sentence of a paragraph serves several purposes: Sometimes it is a transition to the next paragraph and sometimes the author has just finished describing the focus of the paragraph (as in this case). Mr. White feels he has given us six images of early summer days on the farm and we are now ready to move on in the story. He now closes the paragraph with the sentence about Avery (it's still an early summer days image) but it makes us think about what is coming next.

Share a second example from page 43 (the paragraph about the birds) to reinforce topic, supporting sentences, and closing sentence. Look quickly at the second example, but don't linger (unless students are struggling with the structure of a well-developed paragraph: topic, supporting sentences, and closing).

Explore

Have students practice this strategy using this topic sentence: "Lots of changes happen in fall." Ask them: How is this topic sentence broad and inviting of much detail?

Have students work with partners to practice writing supporting sentences that really elaborate on and magnify images of autumn changes. Have students share their sentences and work as a class to sequence and write the paragraph. Ask them what a good closing sentence for this paragraph would be.

Connect

Have students use the mini-lesson experience to revise their fact or fable explanation paragraphs.

➤ Activity Plan 13: A New Bird

Materials

Bird sounds tape used in Activity Plan 4 and Activity Plan 5
Poster board (one 8½-x-11-inch piece per student)

Engage

Play the bird sounds tape to enjoy a variety of calls.

Elaborate

Introduce the "new bird" project. Address the students as follows:

While you are bird-watching you see a bird no one has ever seen before. Use all your knowledge about birds and your "showing not telling" experiences to prepare a scientific journal introducing the bird to the Audubon Society. Be sure to tell interdependence facts (where it lives, the kind of nest it builds, and its food chain), structure facts (its size, color, beak and feet, and song), life cycle stages, and adaptations facts. Draw a colorful picture of the new bird and be sure to give it a unique name. (*Intrapersonal, Verbal/Linguistic, and Visual/Spatial Intelligences*)

Explore

Have students present their birds to the class or a group of invited guests (i.e., another class, parents, community members).

Connect

Address the students as follows:

Evaluate your work during the bird unit. Choose two pieces to save in your portfolio. Think about these questions: Why did you select these pieces for your portfolio? What did you learn about yourself as a writer; as an observer? If you were to continue working on these pieces, what would you change, and why? (*Intrapersonal Intelligence*)

6 *The Polar Express*

Written by Chris Van Allsburg
Illustrated by Chris Van Allsburg
Boston: Houghton Mifflin, 1985

Summary

➤ Late one Christmas Eve a boy boards a mysterious train that takes him on a magical trip to the North Pole. The train is filled with other children dressed in pajamas and nightgowns, and as they race northward they feast on hot cocoa and rich nougat candies. At the North Pole the boy is chosen to receive the first gift of Christmas, and what he wants more than anything is a silver bell from Santa's sleigh. After receiving the bell, the clock strikes midnight, the elves roar their approval, and Santa and his reindeer team climb into the cold, dark polar sky as the children return to the train, where the boy discovers that he has lost the first gift. The sadness of losing the bell turns to joy when the boy discovers a small package left under the tree with a message from Mr. C., "Found this on the seat of my sleigh. Fix that hole in your pocket."

Award Year

➤ 1986

Art Information

➤ Illustrated using oil pastels on pastel papers.

Curriculum Connections

➤ Writing, recalling memories

➤ Activity Plan 1: Sharing the Story

Materials

Christmas bell
Memory pictures (Select a variety of holiday photographs from your experiences and
    place them in a writing journal.)
Caldecott Award poster
Oil pastel crayons (available at art stores)
Pastel paper (available at art stores)
Activity sheet 6.1, Question Chart: Five Ws (one per student)

Engage

Gently ring the bell and introduce the story. Tell the students: This bell reminds a boy
of a magical Christmas memory. Listen to what he tells.

Elaborate

Read the story.

Explore

Ask the students: What words does the author use to help us know that this memory is
magical? How does he show us the memory? (Have students remember words describing the arrival
of the train, riding the train, the trip northward, the North Pole, the first gift and Santa's leave-
taking, loss of the gift, and return of the gift.) What holiday memories are particularly vivid for you?
How does the memory connect with your present circumstances?

Show the photographs you have selected and placed in your writing journal and share
the following information:

Photographs are one way to help recall experiences from the past, and now
that I've placed them in my journal, I can begin to recall and write details
of the memories. Some questions to help me think are the five Ws.

Select one of the pictures in your journal, distribute the five Ws chart to the students, and
invite them to ask you questions about your holiday memory. Share the details sparked by their questions.

Note: Memory writing builds bridges from the past and helps students select and show
parts of themselves through the stories they tell about memorable events in their lives. Autobio-
graphical writing reports the events of life, whereas memory writing adds a deeper layer in which the
writer shows his or her inner feelings and thoughts during the event. Van Allsburg's *Polar Express* reveals
the childlike magic that has stayed with the boy even as a grown man—the ability to truly believe.

The 5 Ws

Who was involved?

What happened?
What was I thinking?
What was it like for me?
What does it represent to me?

When did it happen?

Where was I?

Why would it make a good story?
How did I feel?
Why is it important to me?

➤Activity Sheet 6.1. Question Chart: Five Ws

Connect

Share the Caldecott Award information:

1. As students examine the cover of the book, ask them what special thing they notice. (gold medal) Ask them what the name of the medal is. (Caldecott Award Medal) Ask them why it has been placed on this book. (Some answers may be: The illustrations are special, well done, particularly interesting, exciting, and/or unusual.)

2. Discuss the art techniques used in creating the pictures as follows:

   > Oil pastels are the medium for the illustrations and they create an "otherworldly" feeling that goes right along with the story. Colors are muted and images are fuzzy at the edges. [I particularly like how he illustrated the first view of the hundreds of elves crowding the streets.] Touches of light (from an unseen moon and through the windows of the buildings and the train) and sparse detail emphasize the dark and the shadows and the magic of the experience.

3. Ask two student volunteers to search the poster for the year the story won. (Searching the poster helps students become familiar with the many different titles selected for the award.)

Have students search their photograph albums to select two or three pictures that represent possibilities for memory stories. They should mount the pictures in their writing journals, using the five Ws brainstorming questions (activity sheet 6.1) to recall details of the memories. If students are stumped have them work with partners; partners can look at the pictures and ask questions about what they see. Circulate as students work, giving support and encouragement and modeling the questioning process.

➤Activity Plan 2: Rough Drafting, Revising, Editing, and Publishing—Writing Memory Stories

Materials

Transparency of figure 6.1, Choosing Your Central Focus
Transparency of figure 6.2, Organizing the Memory Information

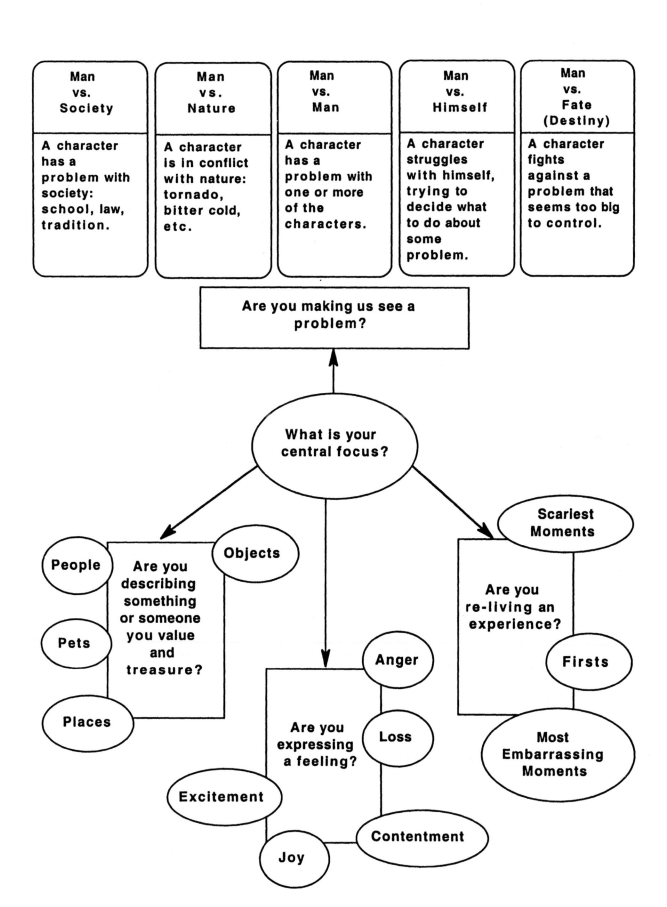

➤ Figure 6.1. Choosing Your Central Focus

The Memory Begins	The Events of the Memory	The Memory Ends

➤ Figure 6.2. Organizing the Memory Information

Engage

Divide the board into three columns labeled "The Memory Begins," "The Events of the Memory," and "The Memory Ends." Have students select a memory story idea, use the elaboration of details information, and organize the information into the three columns (see figure 6.2). (*Logical/ Mathematical Intelligence*)

Elaborate

Review the central focus story chart (figure 6.1); selecting a central focus helps students write with more clarity and direction in rough drafting and evaluate rough drafts more effectively during revision.

Saying Good-Bye

In this picture of my best friend and I, you would never guess that we were saying good-bye, forever I thought. He was moving across the country and I was staying put. We had been best friends since we were two years old, five whole long years of sharing secrets, laughing together, long hours sledding on the hill behind the Catholic Church on the corner, exploring and building forts, especially the Dead-Eye Club where no girls were allowed—not even my mom. He was good at soccer and I played baseball, but that didn't matter.

I remember the first time he spent the night . . . we built a huge house in the dining room with the chairs and the table and lots of blankets and sheets. We both liked to watch Tom and Jerry cartoons, so we pretended to be mice and Mom and Dad were the cats. We even slept in the house. For breakfast he asked for sugar for his cereal (my mom really had to hunt for the sugar), and I was surprised when he used three heaping teaspoons.

One summer we collected toads and used an old aquarium to keep them in. They would bury under the sand to hide and we would dig them up to count and be sure they were still all there. We went bug hunting every day . . . the grasshopper was the most interesting bug we watched the big toad eat. The toad swallowed it in stages and it took a long time. We finally had to let the toads go because school had started and it was hard to find enough bugs. We released them into the back garden and they quickly hopped away.

Best friends don't happen quickly for me. It takes a while to find a new best friend. That's why I'm so looking forward to seeing him again. A year has passed, and he's coming soon and we'll do all the things we used to do and I'll tell him everything that's happened to me. We're still best friends even though we haven't seen each other for a year.

Discuss the central focus of the story. What is the main purpose of the author? (to describe someone who is special and express a feeling of loss) How do we know this person is special?

To help students be clear about the purpose for their memory stories, ask these questions to guide students in choosing the central foci of their memory stories: What do you want your audience to know or learn from your memory story? When you look over your brainstorming column, what words and phrases help you accomplish your purpose? What would you add to your brainstorming columns?

Explore

Have students write their rough drafts, then conference with each other to share what they have written. Conferencing should follow the checklist of questions in activity sheet 6.4. (Give students the activity sheet as a handout or use it as a transparency.) Have students use the information from the conferencing conversations to make revisions in their stories.

Connect

Have students edit (check spelling, capitalization, and punctuation) and publish final copies.

➤ Activity Plan 3: Looking to the Past! Gathering More Writing Ideas

Materials

Memory Starters/Questions (activity sheet 6.2 as a transparency or as a handout)
Expert web (figure 6.3 as a transparency or as a handout)
Accomplishments Brainstorming Chart (activity sheet 6.3 as a transparency or as a handout)
Writing journals

Text continues on page 114.

Memory Starters
The first time I ...
The last time I ...
My scariest memory ...
The silliest thing that ever happened to me ...
The earliest thing I remember ...
I was happiest when ...
My favorite ...
Questions for Elaborating Details
Why did I select this story?
Why is this event important to me?
Why did this story "stick with me"?
What does it say about me?
What was I feeling/thinking during the experience?
What do I want others to know because of hearing this story?

► Activity Sheet 6.2. Memory Starters/Questions

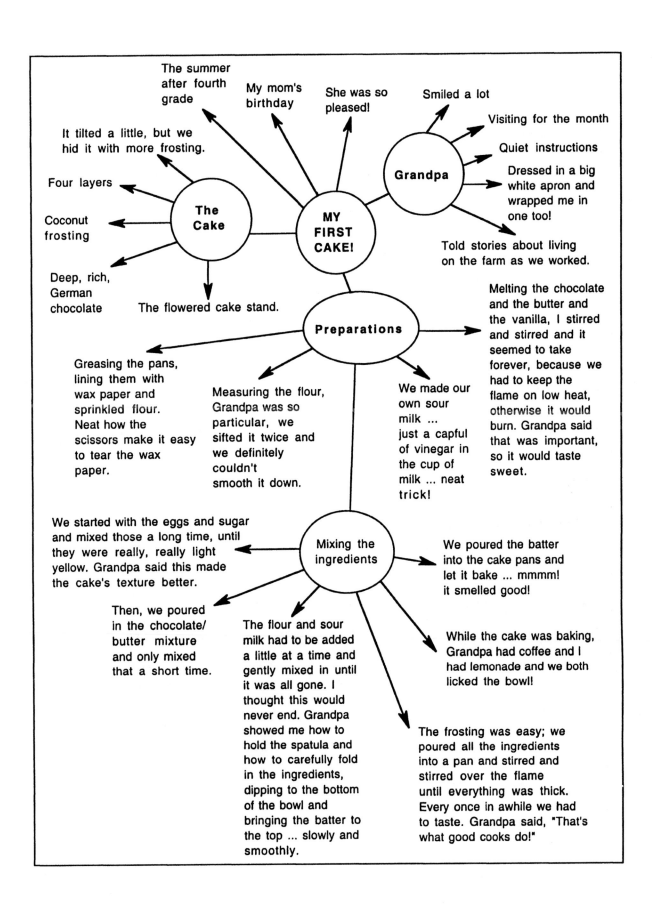

➤ Figure 6.3. Web: I Am an Expert

This Is Me
Now that I'm seven ... When I was six ... During my fifth year ... Now that I'm four ... Because I am three ... When I was two ... By my second birthday ... In the year I was born ...
Questions for Elaborating Details
How do these memories describe who I am today? What are my hopes and dreams for the future? What do I want for this new year of my life? When I am _____(next birthday), I will say this about myself ...

➤ Activity Sheet 6.3. Accomplishments Brainstorming Chart

Conferencing Questions

Are my ideas arranged in the best order?

Can you identify a beginning, middle, and end in my story?

What do you see as my central focus?

What details or other examples should I add?

What should I change?

Engage

Display the memory starters/questions and review them. Ask the students what memories are evoked by these starters. If students have other starters they prefer to use, encourage them to do so. Select one of the memories and add dimension to it by having students ask each other the questions on the handout. (*Intrapersonal, Interpersonal, and Verbal/Linguistic Intelligences*)

Elaborate

Display figure 6.3, Web: I Am an Expert, and review it with the students. Have students brainstorm something they know best (at which they are experts) and begin webs describing everything they know about that topic and how they learned it. Have students reflect on the web and add layers by asking these questions:

- What/who helped you become experts?

- What does this mean for how you like to learn?

- What did you do when you faced an obstacle or continuing became too hard?

- How would you like peers to use this expertise?

Explore

Have students look back at the years of their lives and celebrate the accomplishments. Begin with the most current year and travel back in time to early years; for the early years, encourage students to interview family members. If students can't think of ideas for each year, encourage them to elaborate on what they have written. Use the structure shown in the chart (activity sheet 6.3) to begin describing the memories. Expand the memories with the questions in the chart.

Connect

Give students opportunities to use these prewrite ideas and expand them into published memory stories.

7 *Rapunzel*

Retold by Paul O. Zelinsky
Illustrated by Paul O. Zelinsky
New York: Dutton Children's Books, 1998

Summary

➤ Mr. Zelinksy retells the German folktale from the Brothers Grimm about a young girl named Rapunzel who is locked in a tower by a sorceress when she is twelve. For years she lives alone in the tower, until one day a king's son comes riding through the woods and hears her voice as she sings to the forest birds. His arrival changes Rapunzel's life forever.

Award Year

➤ 1998

Art Information

➤ Illustrated using oil paints.

Curriculum Connections

➤ Fairy tales

➤Activity Plan 1: Sharing the Story

Materials

Six signs (see figure 7.1)
Caldecott Award poster
Tube of oil paint (available at art supply stores)
Small container of odorless turpentine (available at art supply stores)
Paintbrush
Small piece of cardboard to use as a paint palette
One piece of drawing paper

Fairy Tales	
Beginning	"Once upon a time ..." or "Long, long ago ..." or some combination of these words.
Ending	"And they lived happily ever after."
Characters	Characters are often all good or all bad. The good are rewarded and the bad are punished.
Patterns	The number three is a recurring pattern, either in three characters, three events, three tasks, three challenges.
Plot	Stories often begin with commands or promises, which if broken will cause trouble.
Magic	Often include magic which helps or protects the main character.

➤Figure 7.1. Characteristics of Fairy Tales

Engage

Draw an umbrella on the board and write *folklore* on the cap of the umbrella (see figure 7.2). Folklore is the umbrella over a whole group of stories. Ask students: What kinds of stories are folklore stories? Have them brainstorm kinds of folklore; responses may include folktales, fairy tales, animal tales (trickster, pourquoi or tell me why, fables), legends (also includes tall tales if the legends are exaggerated), and myths. Ask students if they know how these stories differ (see figure 7.3) and if they know other characteristics of folklore (see figure 7.4). (*Visual/Spatial and Verbal/Linguistic Intelligences*)

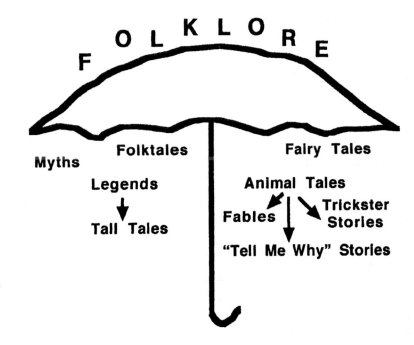

➤ Figure 7.2. Folklore Types

Types of Folklore	Characters	Plot
Myths	Gods and goddesses	Explanation stories: how the world came to be, why humans and animals behave as they do, etc.
Legends	Humans, animals with human behaviors	Stories of the actions of heroic figures; Stories telling about changes in animal and human behaviors and characteristics
Tall Tales	Humans, animals with human behaviors	Stories of the actions of heroic figures, but the solutions result from <u>exaggerated</u> abilities or characteristics.
Fairy Tales	Humans, magical beings	Wonder tales in which the hero or heroine triumphs over great odds.
Fables	Animals with human behaviors	Stories which tell a lesson or a moral.
Pourquoi Tales	Humans, animals	<u>Entertaining</u> stories explaining animal traits or characteristics or behaviors of humans.
Trickster Tales	Wise trickster (animal or human)	Stories showing how a small, defenseless trickster can use his/her <u>mental abilities</u> to outwit a more powerful opponent.
Folktales	Humans, animals with human behaviors	Entertaining stories in which humility, kindness, patience, sympathy, hard work, and courage are rewarded.

➤Figure 7.3. Comparisons of Folklore Stories

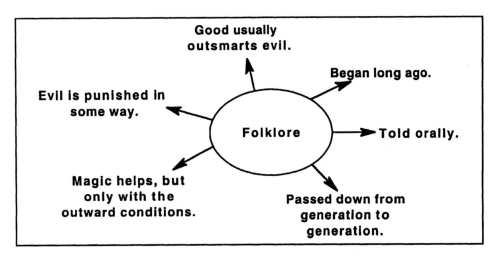

➤Figure 7.4. Characteristics of Folklore

Dramatically retell the following story and invite audience participation whenever you can.

Once upon a time there lived a farmer who had quite a farm; he raised all sorts of crops and quite an assortment of animals, lots of cows, a horse or two, some chickens, oh, and definitely some pigs. The pigs were actually his pride and joy and he made sure that they were well fed and happy.

One evening his grandchildren were visiting and wanted a story. The farmer didn't really have a story, but they begged and begged and wouldn't give up until he settled in the rocking chair, gathered the children around him, and began a story. But what to tell them? He thought for a while and began to talk about himself.

Once upon a time there was a farmer who had a wonderful farm with good crops and lots of animals. Now, his pride and joy were the pigs. They got the best foods and lived in a specially built pen near the barn. One day three of the pigs decided they were not happy and needed a new home; they set off together and soon met a man carrying a load of straw.

The oldest pig said to the man, "Please man, give me that load of straw. I want to build a new home." The man was happy to be relieved of that load of straw and gladly gave it to the pig, and the pig built himself a new shelter. The other two pigs went on their way.

No sooner had the pig settled in his home when along came a . . . (Now, what would most worry a farmer? a fox? a snake? a wolf?) wolf. He smelled that pig and wanted the pig for his dinner.

He knocked on the door and said [in a deep, growly voice], "Little pig, little pig, let me come in."

The pig knew that the wolf was no friend of his and said [have students respond in high piglet voices], "No, no, not by the hair of my chinny, chin, chin!"

The wolf said, "Then I'll huff and I'll puff and I'll blow your house in." Which he did [huff and puff with the students], but the pig was able to escape and run into the woods to find his brothers. The wolf was very upset about losing his dinner and determined that he would find the pig.

The second pig met a man carrying a load of sticks and said to him, "Please man, give me those sticks, so I can build a new home." The man gave him the sticks and soon another house was built. It was not long before the wolf came again. If he couldn't find the other pig, this one would do instead.

He knocked on the door and said [again in a deep, growly voice], "Little pig, little pig, let me come in."

The second pig said [students respond again], "No, no, not by the hair of my chinny, chin, chin."

"Then I'll huff and puff until I blow the house in." Which he did, but the second pig was able to escape into the woods to find his brothers. By this time the wolf was really desperate for a meal and he was determined to find those pigs.

You know the rest of the story. The farmer's grandchildren were so delighted with this story that they asked him to tell it each time they visited. When they grew up, they told their children, and their children told their children and slowly it was passed from generation to generation until it was written down and we have it today.

Fairy tales come from this oral tradition of storytelling and they share some distinctive characteristics (see figure 7.1) Ask the students what they think these are. (Students sometimes need a little prompting but usually say "once upon a time," the happily ever after ending, and the magical elements; help them discover the other three.) Display the signs as each characteristic is identified.

Elaborate

One of the magical elements in the story for today is long hair. Dramatically pose this problem for the students: What if you had long, long, long, long hair? What would be the benefits or the difficulties? Have students use charades to demonstrate the benefits and difficulties instead of speaking their responses. Model this by pretending to use the long hair as a blanket (shiver, then pretend to wrap up in your hair, then smile) or as a jump rope. (*Bodily/Kinesthetic Intelligence*)

Explore

As students listen to the story, have them watch for the six characteristics of a fairy tale (show the story signs from figure 7.1).

Connect

Ask the students how the characteristics are used in the story. Review each one and have students identify connections in the story. Have students speculate about what happened to the sorceress. (Some responses may be: She made another bargain and locked another young girl in the tower, the prince and Rapunzel found her and locked her away, or she died of unhappiness and disappointment.)

Share the Caldecott Award information:

1. As students examine the cover of the book, ask them what special thing they notice. (gold medal) Ask them what the name of the medal is. (Caldecott Award Medal) Ask them why it has been placed on this book. (Some answers may be: The illustrations are special, well done, particularly interesting, exciting, and/or unusual.)

2. Discuss the art techniques used in creating the pictures:

   As I look at the illustrations in the book, I feel as though I could step right into them and become part of the scene because they are so realistic. [Slowly browse several of the pictures.] The colors are also particularly vibrant and rich. What illustrating medium was used to create these pictures? [Browse several pictures and invite speculation; oil paint is the medium.]

   Show the oil paint pigment tube and squeeze a small portion onto the paint palette. Thin the pigment with the odorless turpentine and paint on the drawing paper to show the richness and depth of color. Tell the students that in the endnotes Mr. Zelinsky talks about painting in the Italian Renaissance style with "light falling on tree leaves and billowing drapery." (Browse the story to find examples of the light and to discuss the clothing illustrations, which show lots of folds and depths.)

3. Ask two student volunteers to search the poster for the year the story won. (Searching the poster helps students become familiar with the many different titles selected for the award.)

➤ Activity Plan 2: Expanding Awareness

Materials

Variety of fairy tales (one per student)
A crossword puzzle maker (The crisscross puzzle maker at <http://www.puzzlemaker.com/> is an easy one to use.)
Creative Products Planning Form (activity sheet 7.1; one per student)

Tape recorder, audiotape
World map
Thumbtacks and yarn

Engage

Have students select individual fairy tale titles and use them for independent reading. They will create four products from these independent reading choices: crossword puzzle clues, cinquain poems, creative advertisements, and contributions to an international bulletin board of fairy tales from around the world. Begin with the crossword puzzle clues.

Crossword Puzzle

Use the crossword puzzle-maker to build a class crossword puzzle from the fairy tales students are reading. Have students contribute clues and answers (one per student) based on the fairy tales they are reading. For example, in "Pome and Peel," Peel is turned to (stone), or in "Beauty and the Beast," the two oldest sisters want rich clothes, but Beauty asks for a (rose). (*Verbal/Linguistic Intelligence*)

Elaborate

Help students write cinquain poems as their second products.

Cinquain Poems

Have students use the writing process (prewrite, rough drafting, revision, editing, publishing) to create cinquain poems that describe main characters in each of the tales. For prewrite brainstorming, students should fold papers into fourths to create four idea columns labeled *adjectives, verbs, important events,* and *synonyms* (see figure 7.5). Students scan their books to select and list words and phrases that tell about the appearance and personality of the characters, their actions and involvement in important events, and all the ways the characters can be named.

Adjectives	Verbs
Important Events	**Synonyms**

➤ Figure 7.5. Cinquain Prewrite: Words from the Story

When rough drafting students should take ideas from their brainstorming columns and write cinquain poems, following these directions:

- Line one tells the name of the character.

- Line two lists two adjectives that describe the main character.

- Line three gives three verbs in sequence. (These verbs should relate directly to actions performed by the main character and be listed in the order they happened in the story.)

- Line four is a four- to five-word phrase that describes an important event.

- Line five is a one- to two-word synonym for line one (see figure 7.6).

```
        Character's name _____.

    Two adjectives    _____.

Three verbs (in sequence)_____.

Four- or five-word phrase_____

                    _____.

    One- or two-word synonym_____.
```

➤ Figure 7.6. Cinquain Poem Form

During revision, encourage students to look for repetition and how effectively they have used the words of the author in developing the poem; they should revise the poems so each line gives new information (does not repeat words or ideas) and includes language from the book. This will make the poem more interesting and more reflective of the full story. Editing corrections should check capitalization, spelling, and punctuation. Have students write or type final copies, publish them, and add portraits of the main characters to the published copies. They should then present the poems to the class. (*Verbal/Linguistic and Visual/Spatial Intelligences*) Following are some sample poems.

Prince Sad, determined Traveled, searched, married Tested princess with a pea King	*Ravens* Coal-black, seven Fetched, transformed, returned Their sister saved them. Seven Brothers

Explore

Give students three choices for completing creative advertisements: three-dimensional displays, television spots, or radio interviews. Advertisements should peak interest in the stories, but not give away endings. Preliminary planning starts with completion of the Creative Products Planning Form (activity sheet 7.1). The planning sheet helps students incorporate important, attention-getting details from the story.

Choice 1: Three-Dimensional Displays

The three-dimensional display illustrates an important idea from the story and is accompanied by a descriptive card. For example, to prepare a display on *Puss in Boots*, a student recorded this information on her creative products planning form:

Name: Andrea

Title and Author: *Puss in Boots* by Paul Galdone

Beginning: The old miller dies and leaves the mill to his older sons and a cat to his youngest son.

Setting: Country village in a kingdom

Characters: The miller's son (who was kindhearted and listened to the cat) and Puss (who was clever and had a plan to bring wealth and happiness to himself and his master)

Magic: Puss walks and talks like a human.

Pattern of Three: Puss catches wild game for the king; introduces the miller to the king; and conquers the ogre to bring wealth and happiness to himself and the miller's son.

Ending: The miller's son marries the king's daughter and lives happily ever after. Puss lives contentedly also.

Display: I will show the cat because he is the most important part of the story and really brings all the happiness to the miller's son.

Creative Products: Fairy Tales

Your name_____

Title and Author_____

1. How does your story begin?_____

_____

_____

2. What is the setting of your story?_____

_____

_____

3. Who are your main characters? Tell a little about them.

_____

_____

_____

_____

4. What magical elements are part of your story?

_____

_____

5. What is your pattern of three? _____

_____

_____

_____

6. How does your story end? _____

_____

_____

7. What important part of the story will you show in your creative product?

_____

_____

_____

►Activity Sheet 7.1. Creative Products Planning Form

The student used a stuffed cat and dressed it in boots (back paws) and a "Three Musketeers"-type hat, surrounding the cat with items from the story: a small leather bag, a toddler's shirt and pants, a sickle (crafted from toothpicks and popsicle sticks), and a stuffed mouse. The cat sat in an upright position and held the descriptive card in its front paws. The descriptive card read as follows (*Bodily/Kinesthetic and Verbal/Linguistic Intelligences*):

Puss in Boots

If you were a cat, how would you help your master (the youngest son of a miller) inherit a kingdom and live happily ever after? Puss, dressed in a pair of walking boots (a gift from the miller's son), uses his wits and a small leather bag to capture rabbits and partridges to deliver to the king as special gifts from the Marquis of Carabas (actually the Marquis is the miller's son). He steals the clothes of the miller's son and introduces him to the king as the Marquis of Carabas, but his greatest challenge comes when he meets the ogre. To find out if he saves his own life and brings happiness to the miller's son, read the rest of the story.

Another student displayed a pair of worn ballet slippers and tucked this descriptive card into the display:

Mystery News Flash!

Twelve princesses, wearing long pink dresses covered in yellow hearts and stars, have been sneaking out of a locked room in the castle. The king has announced a reward to anyone who can discover how they leave and where they go. Several men have tried to find the secret but have failed; it is rumored that Peter, the garden boy, may soon tell a story that reveals their secrets. He has been hidden by an invisible cloak, which has allowed him to follow them. Stay tuned for his story or investigate yourself by reading *The Twelve Dancing Princesses*.

Choice 2: Television Spots

Using costumes, dramatic skills, and creativity, have students prepare and dramatize advertisements that might appear on television. A dramatization about *The Amazing Pig* (retold and illustrated by Paul Galdone; New York: Houghton Mifflin, 1981) began with the entrance of a detective who carried a magnifying glass and was dressed in an overcoat and a Sherlock Holmes hat. (*Bodily/Kinesthetic Intelligence*)

The Amazing Pig

The detective pauses center stage and announces to the audience, "I'm a detective and I'm looking for a pig."

Suddenly a stuffed pig on a stick appears from offscreen. The detective walks toward the pig, carefully examines it through the magnifying glass, shakes his head, and says, "Nope, not the right pig. I've been looking all over for this pig."

Another pig arrives from offstage (a student dressed in costume) and the detective walks slowly around the pig and says, "Still not the right pig. I'm looking for an enchanted pig!"

A book is thrown onstage and the detective says, "Oh, yeah, that's it. Forgot to tell you it was a book. It's a good book; it's about three princesses. Their father tells them not to go in a room, but they get so curious that they do and they find out that the oldest one is supposed to marry a king from the West, the second oldest one, a king from the East, and the youngest one is supposed to marry a pig. Later in the future, the pig comes and marries the youngest daughter. Well, she finds out that at night he turns into a beautiful prince, but that's the rest of the book. I think you ought to check it out first."

More stuffed pigs arrive and the detective throws up his hands and walks offstage, shaking his head and grumbling, "That's enough! I'd better go solve another case. No more pigs!"

Another television spot displayed the gymnastic talent of a student; it began with the student dressed in a formal black jacket pretending to be a news announcer.

The Three Sillies

She announced to the audience, "Welcome to the First Edition, the weekly show all about books. We make you cry, we make you laugh, we make you shiver, but most of all we make you want to read . . . great books! Our book for today is . . . " (The student paused, then pulled off the formal black jacket and posed, dressed in mismatched, baggy, crazy clothes. She paused again, stood on her hands.) "Our book for today is *The Three Sillies*" (retold and illustrated by Paul Galdone; New York: Clarion Books, 1981).

Returning to an upright position, she put her hands at her waist and learned forward, "Imagine trying to get a cow up on your roof to eat the grass. That's just what an old woman did and I could not convince her to cut the grass and throw it down to the cow."

"Or have you ever thought of jumping into your trousers?" (She tried to demonstrate what this might be like, by standing on a chair and leaping forward: The first time she pantomimed missing one leg, the second time she tripped and rolled, the third time she tried running and jumping.) "That's what a traveler I met tried every morning. He was so hot and breathless and ready for my advice." (She pantomimed slowly stepping into the trousers and pulling imaginary suspenders up onto her shoulders, finishing by giving the audience a big smile for the success of her advice.)

"Or maybe you were fooled by the reflection of the moon in the pond and gathered the people of the village to help you get it out! I never laughed so hard in my life!" (She pantomimed the laughter, by slapping her knee and holding her sides, and pretending to laugh uproariously.)

"Those are just some of the things that happen in this book." (She showed the book.) "It's a book that is saturated with scenes of silliness that will split your sides with miles of smiles. So if you want to find out who I married and why I was searching for three sillies, read the book." (The student returned to the chair, muttering to herself about trying to jump into the trousers.)

Choice 3: Radio Interviews

Students pretend to be radio talk-show hosts or hostesses and interview characters, authors, or illustrators from the fairy tales. Students must write the interview scripts (giving a lot of attention to open-ended questions), record the interviews on audiotape, plan music, and change their voices for each person speaking. Following is an example from *The Frog Princess*:

An Interview

Music: Russian music plays in the background and slowly fades as the interviewer begins speaking.

Interviewer (*poetic voice*): Fairy tales are cool. Fairy tales will change your world. If reality gets you down, fairy tales are there to take you into another world.

Interviewer (*normal voice*): In our interview today, we meet Prince Ivan, who has been taking a long journey through dark forests in search of his lost magical frog princess. Prince Ivan, do you have a minute to answer some questions?

Prince Ivan (*deep, gravely voice*): Yes, I think I can spare some time.

Interviewer (*normal voice*): Do you know why your princess vanished from your land?

Prince Ivan (*deep, gravely voice*): Yes, I burned her frog skin.

Interviewer (*normal voice*): It sounds like when you burned her frog skin, she died. Is that why she vanished?

Prince Ivan (*deep, gravely voice*): No. No. No. She could take her frog skin off at night and be herself. That's when I burned her frog skin. When she saw what I had done, she turned into a swan and flew out the window and vanished and I've been searching for her since that time. I must find her and tell her I love her.

Interviewer (*normal voice*): How did she become this frog you talk of?

Prince Ivan (*deep, gravely voice*): It was an evil curse, done by her father. She didn't deserve it, he was angry.

Interviewer (*normal voice*): I'm sorry to hear that. What will happen now?

Prince Ivan (*deep, gravely voice*): I will continue to look for her until I find her. It may take years but I won't stop looking.

Interviewer (*normal voice*): Prince Ivan, this is certainly a sad, sad story. We wish you luck in your quest. If you in the audience hear news of a lost frog princess, please call us here, 1-FAIRY-TALES, and tell us your story.

Interviewer (*poetic voice*): Fairy tales are cool. Fairy tales will change your world. If reality gets you down, fairy tales are there to take you into another world.

Music: Russian music becomes louder and then fades out.

Connect

Have students present their creative advertisements. Introduce the bulletin board project.

International Bulletin Board

Display a map of the world on a bulletin board and have students create symbols, questions, and small author cards for their independent reading choices. Place the students' contributions around the map and use yarn and thumbtacks to connect the cards to the countries of origin; countries of origin can usually be found on the title pages, the reverse sides of the title pages, or the book jackets. For the story *The Princess and the Pumpkin* (adapted from a Majorcan tale by Maggie Duff; New York: Macmillan, 1980), one student placed a large orange pumpkin on the board, attached an author card (title, author, country of origin), and listed this question, "How did this pumpkin solve the princess's problem?" Another student drew an impossible box from his Austrian fairy tale, *Dragon Feathers* (by Andrej Dugina and Olga Dugina; Charlottesville, VA: Thomasson-Grant, 1993), extended feathers and an author card from the box, and asked this question, "What would you do with lucky feathers from a dragon?"

➤ Activity Plan 3: Is It Magical?

Materials

Magic wand (dowel covered in glitter and stars)

Engage

Show the "magic wand" and pass it around the class. Brainstorm and list its magical powers. (*Verbal/Linguistic Intelligence*)

Elaborate

Objects with magical qualities are frequently used in fairy tales. Strega Nona (*Strega Nona* by Tomie dePaola; Englewood Cliffs, NJ: Prentice-Hall, 1975) possesses a magic pasta pot that produces all the pasta she needs when she speaks certain words. A small green pea helps a young girl prove that she is a "real" princess ("The Real Princess" by Hans Christian Andersen, in *The Fairy Tale Treasury*, selected by Virginia Haviland; New York: Coward, McCann & Geoghegan, 1972). The bones of a magic fish help change Nomi's life in an African Cinderella tale ("Nomi and the Magic Fish" by Phumla M'bane, in *Cinderella* by Judy Sierra; Phoenix, AZ: Oryx Press, 1992). Finally, a golden goose brings unexpected fortune to a youngest son (*The Golden Goose* by Linda Jennings; Morristown, NJ: Silver Burdett, 1985).

Explore

Have students create a magical objects display by contributing one object each. Each object should be accompanied by a descriptive card identifying the person who uses it, the way it is magical, and the steps for releasing the magic. For example, one student contributed a handkerchief and the descriptive card revealed this information (*Verbal/Linguistic Intelligence*):

> A kind young child may use the handkerchief as a cloak of invisibility; to release the magic, the handkerchief must be waved three times and snapped three times, then dropped slowly to the ground. As soon as the handkerchief touches the ground, the child becomes invisible.

Connect

Have students tour the magical objects museum; as each display is reached, the student who created the display should become a docent and share information about the display.

➤ Culminating Activity Plan

Materials

Activity sheet 7.2, Fairy Tale Prewrite Form (one per student)

Engage

As preparation for writing original fairy tales, use the international bulletin board display (from Activity Plan 2) and the story map components (activity sheet 7.2) to review the plots of various fairy tales. As you ask each question, select two or three stories and recap the information, then record the information on the board or chart paper.

1. What are the settings in these fairy tales?

2. Who are the characters in these fairy tales? Who is evil?

3. What are the problems and goals in these fairy tales?

4. Which stories have the best patterns of three in the events of the story?

5. What magical elements help the main characters in these stories?

6. How do these stories end?

Story Map
Setting
Characters

Problem		**Goal**
	⟷	

Event 1
Event 2
Event 3
Event 4
Resolution

➤Activity Sheet 7.2. Fairy Tale Prewrite Form

Elaborate

Distribute the story maps and use the information from the example that follows to model how to complete the story maps.

Story Map

Setting: A kingdom, far away and long ago.

Characters: Three sons, a dying mother, a poor wizard.

Problem: The queen is dying.

Goal: The boys must save their mother, the queen.

Event 1: The queen falls ill and may die.

Event 2: The brothers hear a voice that tells them about the magic fruit on the tree of youth at Camen's Rock.

Event 3: The oldest brother (who just wanted the kingdom for himself) sets off, meets the poor wizard, refuses to help him, and becomes lost. The middle brother (who also wanted the kingdom for himself) sets off, meets the poor wizard, refuses to help him, and becomes stuck forever in his nighttime camp.

Event 4: The youngest brother (who is pure in heart) sets off, meets the poor wizard, offers him food and a job, and is rewarded with a magic sword and a map.

Resolution: The youngest brother finds the magic fruit, his mother's health is restored, and he is married and lives happily ever after.

Explore

Have students complete their prewrites by developing story maps for their original fairy tales (setting, characters, problem, goal, events, and resolution). Before students begin rough drafting, read the story of "Camen's Rock" to show the development between the story map and the first draft of the story; then have students use the information listed in their story maps to write the first drafts of their fairy tales.

Camen's Rock

by Adam

Once upon a time there was a very sick queen. When her three sons found out that their mother could die, they went to the royal garden one night and sobbed their hearts out.

Soon, they heard a faint voice saying, "Your mother, the queen, is dying. I know how to save her. Empty your pockets where you stand, then I will tell you." Quickly the brothers emptied their pockets. The voice told them the secret. Then the sons went back to the castle for a good night's sleep.

The next day the queen called her three sons to her. As the three brothers came in they bowed to their mother. "Come, come gather around," said the queen in a shaky voice. "It's time to call the royal will makers."

"No need, mother. We have a solution. There is a magic fruit on the Tree of Youth at Camen's Rock," said the oldest brother.

"No!" said the queen, "The magna beast lives there. He is the meanest, fiercest beast in the world."

"I'll take the chance of being killed for you, Mother," said the oldest brother. But he really wanted to destroy the fruit and any hope of his mother living.

"Okay, but be careful, my son," said the queen. Her oldest son just wanted the kingdom for himself. If the queen died he would inherit the whole kingdom and his brothers would have to obey his every command.

The next day he set off for the Tree of Youth. Before he started on his journey he packed five pieces of bread and a container of white wine. On his way he met a wizard. The poor wizard asked, "Do you have any spare food?"

"You do not need anything!" commanded the oldest brother, and he continued on his way.

The angry wizard cast a spell turning the sign that pointed the direction of the fruit in the wrong way. The oldest brother, not knowing the correct route, went in the direction of the sign. Traveling on the wrong road the oldest brother saw something. It was a kingdom of riches. A beautiful princess waved to him from a castle tower. When the oldest brother neared the castle, the wizard made the horse stop. When the oldest brother tried to get off his horse he couldn't. The riches he wanted were just an illusion. He was stuck on the horse wanting the castle and the princess.

Now, two days passed and the middle brother, believing his oldest brother would not return, left to destroy the fruit. He, too, wanted his mother's kingdom. He met the same wizard. The wizard asked the middle brother the same question that he had asked the oldest brother.

"Do you have any food to spare?"

"Why should you have food and drink?" the middle brother said in an angry voice, and he went on his way. When nightfall came he got off his horse and found a place to make camp. He took his ax to chop wood for a fire. But when the ax struck the log it stuck. His hands were stuck, too, for the angry wizard had cast a spell on the middle brother's ax.

When three days passed, the youngest brother went to the queen, "Mother, I believe something terrible has happened to my dear brothers. With your blessings I will go in search of the fruit from the Tree of Youth."

He left the next day. He too met the wizard. The wizard also asked the same question. "Do you have any food to spare?"

"Yes, I do have some food. Will cheese and bread do? I would be happy to share it with you," said the youngest brother.

"Thank you," the wizard said. "I've been wondering, do you know where I could find some work?"

"Yes, you could work for my mother. She is the queen of the Enchanted Valley," the youngest brother replied. "Tell her, her youngest son sent you and she will give you work."

"For your kindness, I will give you a sword for great self-assurance in time of trouble. I will also give you a map to the Tree of Youth so that you can bring back the fruit for your dying mother."

Then the youngest brother followed the map to Camen's Rock and found the tree. No sooner was he about to take the fruit when he saw the magna beast. For a second he forgot to believe in his abilities. Then he remembered the sword the wizard had given him. He swung the sword striking the magna beast. The beast's head rolled off. The youngest son picked the fruit from the tree and joyfully returned home.

Forever and ever the queen lived in good health, as well as the rest of the people in the kingdom. The youngest son married a princess from another kingdom and also lived happily ever after.

When revising, have students check to be sure they have clearly used the six characteristics of a fairy tale (once upon a time beginning, happily ever after ending, good and bad characters, a pattern of three, a command or a promise, and magical elements). Once stories are edited (spelling, capitalization, and punctuation corrections done) and published, gather them into a class book. If photocopying facilities are available, have multiple copies made so each student has a copy.

Connect

Have students share their stories.

8 Sam, Bangs and Moonshine

Written by Evaline Ness
Illustrated by Evaline Ness
New York: Henry Holt, 1966

Summary

➤ When Sam almost loses her cat Bangs and her best friend Thomas, she finally discovers the difference between real and moonshine and learns to live with real. Sam's favorite place for imagining was the ragged old rug on the doorstep, and today when Thomas arrived, Sam traveled on the rug to the moon and sent Thomas racing on his bicycle to the cave behind Blue Rock in search of her baby kangaroo pet and her mermaid mother. What Sam forgot was that the tide rose early and made the trip to Blue Rock dangerous, and the trip became even more dangerous when a sudden thunderstorm rumbled in and brought torrential rains. Thomas is rescued, Bangs returns unexpectedly, and Sam realizes the difference between good moonshine and bad moonshine.

Award Year

➤ 1967

Art Information

➤ Illustrated using line and wash, an inked roller, and a wad of string.

Curriculum Connections

➤ Creative writing, wish poems, lighthouses

➤ Activity Plan 1: Sharing the Story

Materials

Caldecott Award poster
Pen with water-soluble brown or black ink (available at art supply stores)
Paintbrush
Small cup of water
Drawing paper (one sheet)
String (small wad)

Engage

Write these phrases on the board: "Real not moonshine," "Moonshine spells trouble," "Moonshine is flummadiddle," and "Real is the opposite." Ask the students what they mean and why they should be of concern to Sam and her cat Bangs. Invite speculations as a way of sparking interest in the story, but don't worry if they aren't accurate. (*Verbal/Linguistic Intelligence*)

Elaborate

Read the story.

Explore

Discuss the story. Ask the students what Sam finally realizes and what will help her know the difference between good moonshine and bad moonshine.

Connect

Share the Caldecott Award information:

1. As students examine the cover of the book, ask them what special thing they notice. (gold medal) Ask them what the name of the medal is. (Caldecott Award Medal) Ask them why it has been placed on this book. (Some answers may be: The illustrations are special, well done, particularly interesting, exciting, and/or unusual.)

2. Discuss the art techniques used in creating the pictures:

    Wash drawings (like the ones in this story) begin with penned lines, and after the lines are drawn, the brush is loaded with water and quickly washed over the lines, creating the dark and light tones. [Use the water-soluble pen and draw a series of lines on the drawing paper, some close together, some spaced on the page; wet the brush and quickly wash the lines to show the light and dark tones that are created. The opening page of the story is a good example; encourage students to pay close attention to the drawings of Sam, the starfish, the fence posts, and the water. Continue to browse the illustrations to identify examples of the wash technique.]

    How is string used? [Display the wad of string and browse the pictures to identify its use in the illustrations; the picture of Sam's father leaving for his day of fishing (he's waving with one hand and carrying a net with the other) really shows the use of string.] Imagine yourself as the artist, carefully arranging the string on the drawing paper, then rolling an inked roller over it, leaving the imprint of the string.

3. Ask two student volunteers to search the poster for the year the story won. (Searching the poster helps students become familiar with the many different titles selected for the award.)

➤ Activity Plan 2: Creating the Wish Poems

Materials

Thesauruses (one per student or student partnership)
Writing journals

Note: Share the poems on pages 141–42 and have students use the writing process to write their own wish poems. (*Verbal/Linguistic Intelligence*)

Engage

Prewriting

Sam wished her mother was a mermaid and she imagined herself sitting in a chariot drawn by dragons flying to faraway secret worlds. Wish poems imagine what it would be like to be someone or something else.

Have students brainstorm lists of ten wishes (what they might like to be), then choose five of the ideas and explain why they wish to be the objects, animals, insects, people, etc. Ask them what it is about the objects or animals or insects or people that really appeals to them. (See figure 8.1.)

Favorite Wishes	
To be a star	Then, I could hang in the deep, dark sky, wink at astronauts traveling by.
To be a snake	Because, it's a chance to hiss and slither, rattle and warn, curl in a tight circle, and sit in the sun.

➤ Figure 8.1. Wishes

Elaborate

Rough Drafting

Have students use the prewrite ideas and explanations to write poems. Poems should begin with "I wish . . ." or "If I . . . " and should be four lines in length. (See example poems on pages 141 and 142.)

Explore

Revising

The effectiveness of the poems is really based on powerful imagery created by the use of alliteration, simile, and careful word choices.

Use the snake example from figure 8.1 to model revising for careful word choices. List the words from the "rough draft" column and have students dig into their thesauruses to find possible improvements. As improvements are suggested, discuss with students the appropriateness of the choices. Sometimes the suggested synonyms just do not apply to the topic at hand, and you are modeling choosing improvement words that really fit.

Rough Draft	Possible Improvements
slither	zigzag, wind, wriggle
warn	alert, threaten
curl	twist, spiral
tight circle	snug circle

If...

If I could be a kite,

I would glide in the April wind,

my string held tightly in the grip of a small child's hand.

Or maybe I would be a sharp cliff

sticking my face into the world, watching the colors of the

setting sun wash over me.

If I were the rain,

I could patter on the sidewalk or run down the drain.

Some days I would fall like cats and dogs, other days I would be gentle as mist.

Or maybe I would be a daring daffodil

reaching through lingering snow, sunshine sparkling.

Nature Wishes

I wish to be a ladybug,

crawling and flitting, rather than sedately sitting.

I wish to be a cheery cardinal,

perching deep inside a snow-covered pine.

I wish to be a willow, swaying to and fro,

inviting the wind to come play with me.

I wish to be a Canada goose, soaring like an eagle,

north into springtime sky,

anticipating eagerly my favorite nesting spot.

ALLITERATION

Introduce the second revision step: adding alliteration. Evaline Ness uses alliteration in *Sam, Bangs, and Moonshine*: "stranger stories," "curious cargoes," "tallest trees," and "mermaid mother." Revising for alliteration means students must brainstorm words that use the same beginning sounds (setting sun, daring daffodil, sunshine sparkling, sedately sitting, cheery cardinal, springtime sky).

Give students several words and have them use thesauruses to create alliterations. Suggested words include *rocks, wolf,* and *ball* (see figure 8.2).

	Alliteration
Rocks	round rocks, rough rocks, rare rocks, red rocks, or river rocks
Wolf	wandering wolf, watchful wolf, white wolf, wicked wolf, or wild wolf
Ball	bouncing ball or big, blue ball

➤ **Figure 8.2. Alliteration Examples**

SIMILE

Introduce the third revision step: using simile. Revising for similes requires students to create comparison phrases that describe the images in more depth (gentle as mist, soaring like an eagle). (*Verbal/Linguistic and Interpersonal Intelligences*)

Write the word *flower* on the chalkboard. Ask the class to describe the flower and its setting; as students suggest descriptions, write comparison questions next to each idea.

Descriptive Facts	Comparison Questions
red	How red?
tall	How tall?
soft, smooth petals	How smooth are the petals?
butterfly approaching	What comparison would you make to help us understand the movement of the butterfly?

Comparisons build more vivid imagery. In writing poetry, these comparisons are called similes. Similes use *like* or *as* in their structure—soaring like an eagle, fighting like cats and dogs, floating gentle as mist, rain like hammers on a tin roof. Have students develop similes using the flower ideas and comparison questions.

Write these words on the board: *clown, house, tower, apple, lion, baby, sky.* Have students work with partners, choose one of the words, and write similes. When students share their similes, share only the comparison phrases and have the audience guess which word is being described or compared.

Connect

Have students revise their wish poems by adding similes and alliterations and by using the thesaurus to make more interesting word choices.

Editing

Have students complete editing corrections (spelling, punctuation, and capitalization).

Publishing

Have students prepare final copies, either writing or typing them.

➤ Activity Plan 3: Looking into Lighthouses

Materials

Various light sources (candle, flashlight, lantern, lamp)
Keep the Lights Burning, Abbie, episode 37, Reading Rainbow (Lincoln, NE: GPN, 1987)
Beacons of Light Lighthouses by Gail Gibbons (New York: Morrow Junior Books, 1990; a helpful research source)
Lighthouses Watchers at Sea by Brenda Z. Guiberson (New York: Henry Holt, 1995; a helpful research source)

Engage

Slowly light each light source and ask students to analyze which gives the most light (the lamp, particularly if it has a high-wattage bulb) and which would be easiest to flash in code or sequence (the flashlight).

Elaborate

Expand students' introduction to lighthouses by showing the Reading Rainbow episode on lighthouses. Lavar Burton hosts these programs, and each episode features a variety of books and a visit to a real-world setting, in this case a lighthouse and an interview with a lighthouse keeper.

Explore

Place the lighthouse topic choices in a basket; have student partnerships draw assignment choices and begin researching and gathering notes about the topics. Topics for investigation are beach bonfires and tower bonfires (ancient times), Pharos of Alexandria lighthouse, Aime Argand (improvement in candlepower), Augustin-Jean Fresnel, Fresnel lens, Boston Light (first lighthouse in North America), the Statue of Liberty, lightships, Eddystone Rock, Portland Head Light (Maine), Sandy Hook Light (New Jersey), Federal Lighthouse Service, and West Quoddy Lighthouse (Maine). (*Interpersonal Intelligence*)

Connect

Introduce acrostic poems so students can begin to think about how they will write their lighthouse research reports. An acrostic poem is a distinctive, creative way of reporting research notes because it describes the topic and uses the letters of the topic to begin each line. Following are two examples: The first reports information about Eric Carle, the children's illustrator, and the second shares images of beauty.

A Favorite Children's Illustrator

Early in kindergarten, delighted in large sheets of paper, colorful paints, and big brushes.

Raised in America and Germany.

Imagined and illustrated.

Collages of bold and brilliant colors.

Children's books: *The Mixed-Up Chameleon, The Very Hungry Caterpillar,*

All About Arthur, Do You Want to Be My Friend?, and many more.

Received many awards.

Loved to go on long nature walks with his father.

Early job as a graphic designer for the *New York Times* led to story writing and illustrating.

Images of Beauty

Beautiful yellow butterflies float in the spring wind.

Elegant ebony dogs prance in the circus parade.

Adorable white kittens purr softly as they settle into sleep.

Unusual striped bumblebees sleep on the roses in my garden.

Tiny orange marigolds soak in the sun.

Young fluffy lambs gambol in the green meadow.

➤Activity Plan 4: Creating Acrostic Poems

Engage

Two prewriting strategies help student partnerships write the lighthouse poems: creating a list of bridge words and writing a class poem using a character from the book.

Prewriting

Work together as a class to brainstorm a list of bridge words (prepositions, conjunctions, and other words) that can be used when students are writing acrostic poems. The bridge words help when students are stumped and can't think of a word that begins with a certain letter. Students can browse dictionaries, encyclopedias, and language arts books to help add words to the list (see figure 8.3).

Use topics from the book (Bangs the cat, Sam, or Moonshine the gerbil) to model writing the poems. Ask students to list information from the book about one of the characters, e.g., Moonshine. (a gerbil; hops on its back legs; looks like a miniature kangaroo; has large eyes, a tiny head, and a long tail like a lion's; a gift for Thomas; arrived on an African banana boat; it delights Sam) Have students use the gathered facts and the bridge words list to write the acrostic poem together. Following is an example from a second-grade class. (*Verbal/Linguistic Intelligence*)

Moonshine is a gerbil who arrived

On an African banana boat. When Sam

Opened her eyes the

Next morning after the terrible storm,

She couldn't believe what she saw.

Hopping toward her was a baby kangaroo, she thought.

It had a long tail like a lion's, a tiny head, and huge eyes.

Now she could really surprise Thomas and maybe

Even make up for the trouble she had caused; she would give the gerbil to him!

Bridge Words	
A	and, an, after, about, around, as
B	because, before, between, by, but, both
C	could, can
D	down, during
E	each, every, even, except, either
F	for, from
G	go, going, get
H	he, his, her
I	in, into, instead of, if, in addition to
J	just
K	key, keep
L	like
M	most, more
N	none, near, not, neither, nor, never, next, now
O	on, over
P	please, put
Q	quickly, quite
R	rarely
S	so, some, since
T	to, through
U	under, upon, unless, until
V	very
W	with, without, where, while
Y	yet

➤ Figure 8.3. Bridge Words

Elaborate

Rough Drafting

Have students begin rough drafts when their research notes are thorough and complete. Line one of the acrostic poem should name the assignment topic and give an important fact. Encourage students to select the fact they wish to use, then refer to the bridge words list to make the fact fit the line they need; this will avoid the frustration of looking for research facts that begin with the letters they need. For example, when writing an acrostic poem about the lighthouse at Pharos, students might begin the poem with the following lines. (*Verbal/Linguistic and Interpersonal Intelligences*)

P haros of Alexandria was an ancient lighthouse built in the

H arbor of Alexandria, Egypt, by Alexander the Great

The third line must begin with the letter "a"; the second-grade students wanted to use the fact that the lighthouse was one of the Seven Wonders of the World. Students reviewed the bridge words list and used "and" to begin the next line:

A nd it became known as one of the Seven Wonders of the Ancient World.

Because the research topics are too long as titles for the acrostic poems, shorten the topics (examples follow):

Research Topics	Acrostic Poem Titles
beach bonfires and tower bonfires	BONFIRES
Pharos of Alexandria lighthouse	PHAROS
Aime Argand	ARGAND
Augustin-Jean Fresnel	FRESNEL
Fresnel lens	FRESNEL LENS
Boston Light	BOSTON LIGHT
The Statue of Liberty	LIBERTY STATUE
Lightships	LIGHTSHIP
Eddystone Rock	EDDYSTONE
Portland Head Light	PORTLAND
Sandy Hook Light	SANDY HOOK
Federal Lighthouse Service	LIGHTHOUSE SERVICE
West Quoddy Lighthouse	WEST QUODDY

Following is an example of an acrostic poem using research notes for the Boston lighthouse:

Boston Light was the first lighthouse built in North America. It was placed

On Little Brewster Island in 1716 to help

Ships sail carefully in and out of Boston harbor.

This lighthouse used a wick lamp that burned whale

Oil or fish oil. The lighthouse keeper's work

Never stopped, because the lamp wick had to be trimmed to keep it from smoking. Up and down the

Long, winding stairs the keeper walked to keep the lamp shining brightly.

In stormy weather, the fog rolled in, and

Great waves crashed on the island, and sometimes the keeper would

Have to rescue shipwrecked sailors

Tossed by the sea.

Explore

Revising

Reviewing poem lines for more complex sentence structures is a way to be thorough in integrating research notes. Students should review their research notes to identify facts that haven't been used, then look at the bridge words list to find a way to add these notes to the lines of the poem they have already constructed. For example, the Boston Light poem could be revised to add the Revolutionary War fact and the facts about fuel sources:

Ships sail carefully in and out of Boston harbor. The British destroyed Boston Light during

The Revolutionary War, and another lighthouse was built on the island in 1783. Whale

Oil and oil from fish and lard fueled the lamp in the lighthouse. The lighthouse keeper's work

Editing

Have students use computers to type the acrostic poems, making sure to enlarge the first letters of each line so that the topic stands out. Remind them to make editing corrections (spelling, punctuation, and capitalization) before printing final copies.

Connect

Publishing

Create a visual timeline of the history of lighthouses by displaying poems in chronological order and having students add illustrations of their topics (see figure 8.4).

Tour the timeline and have students share their poems. (*Visual/Spatial and Logical/ Mathematical Intelligences*)

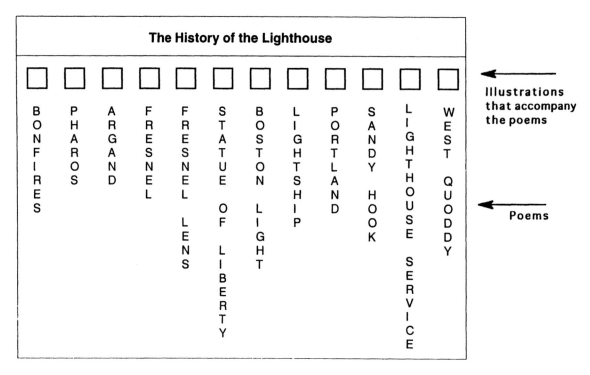

➤ Figure 8.4. Lighthouse Display

9 *Snowflake Bentley*

Written by Jacqueline Briggs Martin
Illustrated by Mary Azarian
Boston: Houghton Mifflin, 1998

Summary

➤ The plaque on the monument says "Snowflake" Bentley, Jericho's world famous snowflake authority. This story shares the life and work of Wilson A. Bentley, a Vermont farmer who spent years developing his technique of micro-photography and used the technique to reveal the structures of snowflakes, publishing his pictures in a book entitled *Snow Crystals*.

Award Year

➤ 1999

Art Information

➤ Illustrated using woodcuts, hand tinted with watercolors.

Curriculum Connections

➤ Report writing

➤ Activity Plan 1: Sharing the Story

Materials

Snowflake Bentley plaque (See figure 9.1; mount this figure on construction paper and heavy-duty cardboard to make it look like a plaque; laminate it if you have access to laminating film.)

Prefolded paper in preparation for making snowflakes:

- eight-pointed snowflake (Fold a square piece of paper diagonally in half; fold in half again twice more.)

- six-pointed snowflake (Fold a square piece of paper in half; fold it in half twice more.)

Scissors
Blue or black construction paper (one sheet per student)
Glue
Rubber stamp
Ink stamp pad
Small, sharp knife
Watercolor pigment (available at art supply stores)
Small paintbrush
Caldecott Award poster

Engage

Display the plaque and invite predictions from the students: What is a snowflake authority? Refocus question: What would you have to do to be a snowflake expert?

Elaborate

Introduce and read the story. As students are listening to the story, ask them to think about why Mr. Bentley is an expert on snowflakes.

Explore

Discuss the story: Why is Mr. Bentley considered an expert on snowflakes? What were some of the challenges he faced as he tried to learn about snowflakes? (Some responses may be that they melt too quickly; they are tiny and it's hard to see the structure unless you have a microscope or special camera; the microscope camera is very expensive; it takes a long time to learn how to take pictures that show the snowflake; he had to work in the cold.) Ask students to think about their own strengths and interests and to share how they are experts in their own lives. (Responses may include sports accomplishments, artistic talents, and hobbies.) As students share, pose questions that encourage them to share how they have become experts in these areas. (*Verbal/Linguistic Intelligence*)

TO

SNOWFLAKE
BENTLEY

JERICHO'S WORLD
FAMOUS
SNOWFLAKE
AUTHORITY

▶ Figure 9.1. Snowflake Bentley Plaque

Address the students as follows:

We learn in the book that Mr. Bentley expected to find whole snowflakes were the same, but he never did; no one design was ever repeated. We can't test his theory, but let's use these prefolded paper shapes to make our own snowflakes and see how they are different. [Have students choose a pre-folded paper and begin to cut and design their own snowflakes; when they have finished cutting, help them carefully unfold the shapes and glue them to blue or black construction paper backgrounds. They only need dabs of glue in three or four places, and it's okay if the snowflakes are not completely flat on the background papers. Display the snowflakes and let students discuss the variety and the designs.] (*Visual/Spatial Intelligence*)

Connect

Share the Caldecott Award information:

1. As students examine the cover of the book, ask them what special thing they notice. (gold medal) Ask them what the name of the medal is. (Caldecott Award Medal) Ask them why it has been placed on this book. (Some answers may be: The illustrations are special, well done, particularly interesting, exciting, and/or unusual.)

2. Discuss the art techniques used in creating the pictures:

   Mary Azarian is the artist who created the illustrations in the book; she used woodcuts and hand tinted them with watercolor paints. [Dip the rubber stamp in the ink and make a print; carefully tint the open spaces in the print with watercolors.] The artist carved her designs from wood, printed them, then added color. [Browse the illustrations to note textures of the wood, particularly noticeable on and in the buildings, and the floors and walls of the rooms, and remark on colors. Also point out how she illustrated the hair of each character.]

   Another unusual technique in the book is the framing on each page: Some pages are separated into two distinct events, while other pages have double-page illustrations and the black border captures the entire scene. Some pages (where additional biographical information is included) have snowflake borders, other pages do not. [Show some examples of each.]

3. Ask two student volunteers to search the poster for the year the story won. (Searching the poster helps students become familiar with the many different titles selected for the award.)

➤ Activity Plan 2: Scenes of Vermont

Materials

Map of the United States

Transparency of figure 9.2

Research time in the library (Schedule time in the library for the students to research their Vermont topics; they will probably need two sessions.)

Transparency and multiple copies of the Information-Gathering Grid (activity sheet 9.1; if it is possible, copy the two pages of the information-gathering grids front and back, rather than on two sheets of paper.)

Transparency of an index page

Transparency and multiple copies (one per student) of the citing sources guidelines (figure 9.3)

Transparency and multiple copies of the Book Page (activity sheet 9.2; make extra copies of this page so students can begin again if they aren't satisfied with first attempts.)

Engage

Have students locate Vermont on a map of the United States and think about what it would be like to live there. You know one characteristic of Vermont from reading the book about Mr. Bentley: It has long, snow-filled winters. Ask the students what other attractions of the state might be. Have students make predictions based on the book and its location in the United States; don't worry if the information isn't correct.

Elaborate

For a prewriting exercise, display the transparency listing the topic choices (see figure 9.1) and introduce the project, making an "ABCs of Vermont" book. Review the topic choices and encourage students to select one or two ideas they would like to explore; have students select topic choices. (Some of the topics may be difficult to find information on or may not have obvious connections to Vermont, so students will need to do some searching; for example, James Sargent is an inventor who devised locks, semaphore signals, and automatic fire alarms; Rudyard Kipling married a woman from Vermont and while he lived in Vermont wrote *The Jungle Book*; Brigham Young was born in Vermont but most of his contributions concern Utah; the Vermont State House topic could easily include information about Montpelier, the state capital; and the University of Vermont could be broadened to include education in Vermont. The "X" topic is a free-choice topic, and the student who selects this choice should find something to share about Vermont that is not covered in the other topics. The "Zoom" topic is a geographical location choice, showing where in the United States Vermont is found, what states and countries surround it, its longitude and latitude, and maybe even a physical map.)

Text continues on page 161.

ABCs of Vermont: Topic Choices
Algonquian tribes
Burlington
Champlain, Samuel de
Deer and other animals of Vermont
Ethan Allen
Forests
Green Mountain State
Hermit thrush
Industry in Vermont
James Sargent (inventor)
Kipling, Rudyard
Lake Champlain
Marlboro Music Festival
New England Village in Shelburne
Old Constitution House
Presidents from Vermont
Quaries of granite
Rivers of Vermont
Snow skiing
Tapping the maple trees
University of Vermont
Vermont State House
White Mountains
X marks the spot ... (free choice)
Young, Brigham
Zoom to Vermont (its location)

➤ Figure 9.2. ABCs of Vermont: Topic Choices

Topic:	Source #1:	Source #2:
Question #1:		
Question #2:		

➤ Activity Sheet 9.1. Information-Gathering Grid

Possible sources of information:

Citing my Sources

Source #1:

Source #2:

▶ Activity Sheet 9.1. Information-Gathering Grid (*cont.*)

Citing Sources

Book
Author's last name, first name. <u>**Title of the Book,**</u> **copyright date, page numbers.**
Facklam, Margery. <u>Bees Sing, Birds Dance,</u> 1992, pages 34-37.

Magazine
"Title of the Article in the Magazine," <u>**Name of the Magazine,**</u> **Month, year, page numbers.**
"Scorpions," <u>Ranger Rick,</u> July, 1992, pages 12-14.

Encyclopedia
"Title of the Article in the Encyclopedia," <u>**Name of the**</u>
<u>**Encyclopedia**</u> **(Copyright Date), volume letter, page numbers.**
"Wolves," <u>New Book of Knowledge</u> (1992), volume W, pages 364-368.

Electronic Database
"Title of the Article in the Database," <u>**Name of the Database,**</u> **copyright date.**
"George Washington," <u>Grolier's Electronic Encyclopedia,</u> 1992.
"Tiger," <u>Mammals,</u> 1995.

Audiovisual Materials (filmstrips, videos, etc.)
<u>**Name of the Material**</u> **(Kind of Material), copyright date.**
<u>Rocks and Minerals</u> (Video), 1991.

World Wide Web
"Title of page or document," Date of document. Online. address.
"Speeches of the President," December 12, 1996. Online.
http://www.whitehouse.gov.

E-Mail
Author of e-mail message. "Subject line of message,"
E-mail to recipient's name. Date of message.
Gibson, Rob. "Fan Mail," E-mail to Madonna, January 27, 1997.

▶Figure 9.3. Guidelines for Citing Sources

Picture of the Topic

_____

_____

_____

_____

_____

➤ Activity Sheet 9.2. Book Page

Brainstorm questions for research, narrow the questions to two, and set up the information-gathering grids (use the transparency of activity sheet 9.1 to model how to prepare the grids). Have students explore these questions: What is it? Why is it important to Vermont? How is it connected to Vermont?

Brainstorm possible sources of information and have students list the possibilities on the reverse sides of the information-gathering grids. Sources include books, magazines, encyclopedias (print and electronic), and Internet sites. Have students evaluate the suggestions to pick two possible starting points. Ask the following questions to encourage this kind of thinking: What source would be a reliable starting point and would easily give you the information you need? Which source will be most helpful and help you easily answer your questions?

Display the transparency of the index page and review its use: What page would give you information about . . . ? (Add a topic selection from the index page.) How would you find information about . . . ? (Choose another topic selection.) Continue this process until you are confident students understand how to use the index. Ask the students: What do you notice about the order of the topics on this page? (alphabetical) Why is the index an important starting point? (It takes you right to where you can find the information you need.) Where is the index located in a book? (back of the book) Where is the index located in an encyclopedia? (separate volume) Where is the index located in an electronic encyclopedia? (using search or find and typing in the topic)

Display the transparency showing how to cite sources (see figure 9.3) and review this process. Students should use the appropriate boxes on the information-gathering grids to list the titles of the resources they use to answer their questions. They should use the reverse sides to cite the sources, using the citing sources guidelines. Model this process of citing sources so students understand the importance of each piece of information and the punctuation. Have students use a book from their desks/cubbies and follow along as you help them write the citation:

1. Find the title page.

2. Write the author's name: last name, comma, first name, period.

3. Write the title of the book; be sure to capitalize the important words and underline the title. Follow the title with a comma.

4. Turn to the back of the title page and find the copyright date for the book. The copyright date tells when the book was printed. Follow this with a comma.

5. If you read one page of information, write the word *page*; if you read more than one page of information, write the word *pages*. Then write the page numbers you read; for example, if you read pages four through eight, you would write "pages 4–8" and follow that information with a period.

Move to the library and begin the research. Circulate as students work to encourage them, help them find effective sources, and reinforce using the indexes to locate information. (*Verbal/Linguistic Intelligence*)

Explore

Rough Drafting

As with writing stories, report leads are important beginnings for writing the reports. The opening paragraph should hook the interest of the reader and introduce and tell facts about the topic. Three ways to provide this catchy beginning include:

1. Starting with a question: Did you know that Vermont is a wonderful place for a skiing vacation?

2. Starting with a dramatic statement: Relive the early pioneer days in Vermont . . . come visit Shelburne Village.

3. Starting with a description: Forests of maple trees stretched as far as the eye could see, each one waiting to be tapped for the spring maple syrup harvest.

Have students collaborate with peers to develop leads for their topics. Leads should be followed by information describing the topic. The second paragraph should include the information from the second question, why this topic is important to Vermont. (*Interpersonal and Verbal/Linguistic Intelligences*)

Revising

Have students exchange papers and have partners read first drafts aloud to check for clarity and details. Encourage students to check their information grids to be sure they have included as much information from their notes as they can.

Editing

Have students check for spelling, punctuation, and capitalization errors. They should pay close attention to names of places and be sure these are spelled correctly and begin with capital letters. Remind them to check for ending punctuation.

Connect

Publishing

Display the transparency of the Book Page (activity sheet 9.2) and show students how to record their information (see figure 9.4).

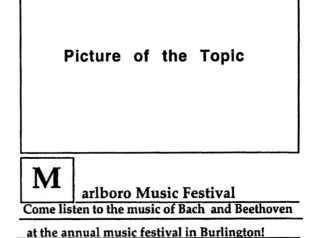

➤ Figure 9.4. Sample ABC Page

The small box should hold the letter of the alphabet featured on the page, followed by the rest of the topic. Students should write their information beginning on the second line.

Have students use separate sheets of paper to plan and sketch their illustrations. Final versions of the illustrations should be sketched and colored in the larger boxes on the page. Encourage neatness, careful use of color, and attention to detail.

Gather the pages into a book and develop title and cover pages. Students who complete their individual pages can be invited to sketch pictures for the title and cover pages (see figure 9.5 for a sample). (*Visual/Spatial and Verbal/Linguistic Intelligences*)

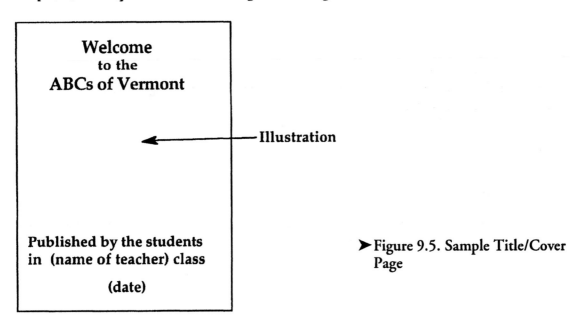

➤ Figure 9.5. Sample Title/Cover Page

Present the book to the class and ask each student to show and read his or her page as you share the book.

➤ Activity Plan 3: Photo Essays

Materials

Snowflake Bentley by Jacqueline Briggs Martin

Photo essay: a selection of photographs telling the story of an event in your life (A vacation, a birthday party, a family reunion, or some other occasion; mount each picture on a separate sheet of paper and write a one- or two-sentence caption for each.)

Transparency and multiple copies of the Storyboard Planning Sheet (Activity sheet 9.3; students will need one planning sheet if the photo essay is a class project or many copies each if it is an individual or collaborative group activity.)

Transparency and multiple copies of the information-gathering grid (Activity sheet 9.1; if possible, copy the two sides of the information-gathering grid front and back, rather than on two sheets of paper.)

Transparency and multiple copies (one per student) guidelines for citing sources (figure 9.3)

Transparency of the interviewing guidelines (figure 9.6)

Camera

Note: Explore options before beginning this project:

1. Disposable cameras are readily available at most discount stores and are inexpensive and easy to use, but the cost of film developing must also be considered.

2. Digital cameras are more expensive but are not hard to use and do not require additional money for film developing because pictures can be printed via the computer. Check in your school district to see if you can borrow a camera during your photo essay unit.

3. Connections with school programs offering photography classes can also solve the problem of film developing costs because students in these classes can develop the photographs for your students.

4. A letter to parents asking for donations or assistance in this project is another possibility; parent volunteers may wish to bring cameras and mentor students as they gather pictures.

5. Hand-drawn pictures and images downloaded from the Internet are additional choices; be sure students cite their sources if they download images from the Internet and make sure they are aware of copyright issues.

Text continues on page 167.

Storyboard no.:	Photo Essay Topic:
Page Title:	Producer/s:

Picture   Idea

Text

Interviewing Guidelines

Before the Interview

1. Write your interview questions.

2. Plan and practice your introduction.
   In your introduction you should tell who you are and where you go to school, then explain your project and arrange a time for the interview.

3. Gather the supplies that you will need.
   Take your questions, pencils, and a notebook. You might want to use a tape recorder to tape the interview if you are interviewing in person.

During the Interview

1. Introduce yourself again.

2. Ask your questions and take notes.

3. If you don't understand an answer, ask for more information.

4. When you are finished, be sure to say "thank you."

After the Interview

1. Read through your notes or listen to the tape to be sure you understand everything. Make changes and additions if you see the need.

2. Include the interview information in your photo essay.

➤ Figure 9.6. Interviewing Guidelines

Engage

Share the photo essay you assembled and describe how the photos and captions bring the event to life. Display *Snowflake Bentley* and tell students that Mr. Bentley created a different kind of photo essay in his book, *Snow Crystals,* when he gathered picture after picture of individual snowflakes to show their universal hexagonal shapes and infinite number of lovely designs. Ask them why they think photo essays are engaging and fun to read. (Answers will vary.)

Elaborate

Many topics provide opportunities for effective photo essays: animals, people and their jobs or hobbies, a celebration of favorite activities and events from the school year for a particular class, ecology issues, healthy eating recommendations, sports, and so forth.

Photo essays can be class projects (my community and our year in pictures are examples of a whole class effort), individual assignments, or collaborative group activities (animals, people and their jobs or hobbies, ecology issues, healthy eating recommendations, and sports work either way).

As a prewriting exercise, select a topic and have students brainstorm ideas for photo essays. Figure 9.7 lists some possibilities.

Once students have selected a subject, their next task is information gathering. Have students use the Information-Gathering Grid (activity sheet 9.1) to list questions they want to research. For example, their questions for a photo essay on an animal might include: What is its cycle of life? Where does it live? How does it survive in its habitat? What does it look like? For an essay about an inventor, their questions might be: What are early life facts? What are his or her inventions? How are these inventions used in everyday life today? Questions for information gathering for "our year in pictures" might be: What was the event? Why was it special? If students are working with partners or in collaborative groups, have them discuss how they will work on the questions; they can all work on all the questions but use different sources, or they can divide the questions.

Brainstorm possible sources of information and have students list the possibilities on the reverse side of the information-gathering grids. Sources include books, magazines, encyclopedias (print and electronic), Internet sites, and interviews. Have students evaluate the suggestions to pick two possible starting points. Ask them the following questions to encourage this kind of thinking: Which source would be a reliable starting point and would easily give you the information you need? Which source will be most helpful and help you easily answer your questions? If the topic offers real-life connections to today, encourage students to think about interviewing; for example, if the topic is animals, they could interview veterinarians or zoo employees; if community helpers, police or fire department employees; if sports, coaches or trainers.

Display the transparency showing how to cite sources (see figure 9.3) and review this process. Students should use the appropriate boxes on the information-gathering grids to list the titles of the resources they use to answer their questions. They should use the reverse side to cite the sources, using the citing sources guidelines. Model this process of citing sources so students understand the importance of each piece of information and the punctuation; use an encyclopedia article as your source. Have students follow along as you help them write the citation:

Brainstorming Examples

<u>Animals</u>: Essays can feature animals found in certain ecosystems (prairie, ocean, forest) or endangered animals of your state, and can focus on such concepts as cycle of life, adaptation, interdependence, structures.

<u>People and Their Jobs or Hobbies</u>: Essays can feature community helpers, inventors, careers, school people and can focus on a day in the life of that person.

<u>My Community</u>: Students can take walking tours of the community and use the photo essay to show goods and services, entertainment, and government in the community.

<u>Our Year in Pictures</u>: Students can review the year's activities: field trips, guest speakers, memorable units, and accomplishments.

<u>Ecology Issues</u>: Essays can focus on how to recycle, how to save energy or how to preserve wetlands, clean water resources, endangered wildlife.

<u>Healthy Eating</u>: The essay can explain the nutrition pyramid and show healthy meals based on the pyramid.

<u>Sports</u>: Students can select a sport and show equipment, movements in the sport, and rules for sportsmanship.

➤ Figure 9.7. Brainstorming Ideas

1. Begin with quotation marks and write the title of the article; close the title with a comma and quotation marks.

2. Write the title of the encyclopedia; be sure to capitalize the important words and underline the title. Follow the title with an open parenthesis.

3. Turn to the back of the title page and find the copyright date for the encyclopedia. Write the date and then a close parenthesis, followed by a comma.

4. Write *volume* and follow it with the volume letter of the encyclopedia, followed by a comma.

5. Write the page or pages and follow this with the page numbers you read. Close the citation with a period.

Display the transparency of the interviewing guidelines (see figure 9.6) and review this process. Role play the introduction and invite a student to introduce himself or herself and explain his or her project.

Schedule time for information gathering. Remind students to notice photograph/picture possibilities as they gather information.

Explore

Rough Drafting

Give students several days to gather information, then model the process of using the information to construct the photo essay:

1. Distribute the Storyboard Planning Sheet (activity sheet 9.3) and have students organize the sequences of their photo essays and complete heading information:

   - The photo essay topic: List the overall subject, e.g., prairie dogs, the library, playing baseball.

   - The producer: Write the name(s) of the students who have chosen the topic.

   - Page title: Have students review their questions to identify key words; e.g., from the animal questions, key words might be *cycle of life, habitat, survival, appearance.* A second step in identifying page titles is to review the information students have gathered to determine how many storyboard pages will be devoted to each key word; e.g., in the animal photo essay, a student might set up these storyboard titles: "Cycle of Life 1" (how it grows), "Cycle of Life 2" (adulthood), "Habitat 1" (location), "Habitat 2" (home), "Survival 1" (food chain), "Survival 2" (adaptations), and "Appearance." The student would write these titles on seven different storyboard sheets; an eighth storyboard sheet would say "Cover Page" and a ninth storyboard sheet would say "Ending Page and Sources."

   - Storyboard number: Have students decide the sequences of their photo essays and number the storyboard planning sheets. The cover sheet will obviously be storyboard sheet 1; in the animal example, the student might have the appearance sheet second, the habitat sheets third and fourth, the life cycle sheets fifth and sixth, the survival sheets seventh and eighth, and the ending/source sheet ninth.

2. Have students review their research notes and write the text that accompanies each page of the photo essay.

3. Have students plan the photographs/pictures that will illustrate each page of the essay. Remind them to review their notes for the possibilities they have listed. Schedule time for gathering the photos or illustrations; once they are gathered, place them on the appropriate planning page.

Revising

Have students share their storyboard planning sheet with partners. They should read each page of information to make sure the facts are clear and easy to understand. Discuss how the pictures/photos make the information real and exciting. A student may also wish to change the sequence of the essay after reviewing it with a partner; remind them to change the storyboard numbers if they do this.

When text is set, have students plan cover and ending pages. Encourage them to be creative in composing their titles; e.g., "Life As a Prairie Dog" or "The World of Thomas Edison" or "Our Year in Pictures"; ending pages should close with a list of resources. Have students select photographs or pictures for the title pages.

Editing

Have students check for spelling, punctuation, and capitalization errors.

Connect

Publishing

If computer lab time is available, schedule time for students to type their photo essay pages, otherwise have them print or write final copies. After text is printed or written, have students add their photos and/or pictures.

Schedule a celebration time, invite parents, and have students share their photo essays.

10   *Time of Wonder*

Written by Robert McCloskey
Illustrated by Robert McCloskey
New York: Viking Press, 1957

Summary

➤ Robert McCloskey celebrates his love for the Maine islands as he tells the story of a long summer vacation filled with foggy mornings, clear sailing among the islands, satisfying afternoons swimming and building sand castles, starry nights, and the roar of a hurricane.

Award Year

➤ 1958

Art Information

➤ Illustrated using casein.

Curriculum Connections

➤ Poetry, celebrating the seasons

➤ Activity Plan 1: Sharing the Story

Materials

Globe

Drawing paper, one sheet per student

Illustrating materials (markers, crayons, chalk, colored pencils)

Clothesline and clothespins (Completed illustrations of the students' memorable summer experiences are best displayed in one long line. If the clothesline/clothespin idea doesn't work for you, choose a wall where the pictures can be hung in one long row at eye level.)

Caldecott Award poster

Paintbrush

Tube of casein pigment, available at art supply stores (This is an older type of pigment, but most art supply stores still stock a small selection of colors; its base is milk curds, it dries like an acrylic, and it mirrors the effect of watercolor paints.)

Engage

Twirl the globe and have students imagine a spot where they might wish to travel for a summer vacation. Encourage them to give reasons for their choices.

Elaborate

Introduce and read the story. The children in this story would probably pick the islands off the coast of Maine as a vacation spot. Ask the students: As you listen to the story, what are reasons the children love summers in Maine? Why is this summer vacation a time of wonder for them?

Explore

Discuss the book. Ask the students: Why is this summer in Maine special for the children? What do they enjoy? (rain coming across the islands, foggy mornings that melt into sunshine, sailing in the cove, spending the day swimming and diving off the point of the island, building sand castles, starlit nights, getting ready for the coming weather, huddling close together safe from the storm, exploring and discovering unexpected treasures after the storm, even leave-taking and a farewell look at the waves and sky) What summer experiences are special to the students? What summertime activities are "time of wonder" experiences for them?

Connect

Share the Caldecott Award information:

1. As students examine the cover of the book, ask them what special thing they notice. (gold medal) Ask them what the name of the medal is. (Caldecott Award Medal) Ask them why it has been placed on this book. (Some answers may be: The illustrations are special, well done, particularly interesting, exciting, and/or unusual.)

2. Discuss the art techniques used in creating the pictures (if students become restless with the page-by-page reexamination of the illustrations, select a few that you really want to share):

   • Pages 6–7: Point out the shades of blue in the water, the deep, deep blue of the foreground water gradually fading to sky blue with a hint of yellow in the middle distance. Tell the students to note the dark undersides of the clouds and how McCloskey has shadowed the land below.

   • Pages 12–13: Point out the reflective quality of the water and the pale green that was used to create the foggy morning. Even the children are muted by the foggy morning.

   • Pages 16–17 and pages 18–19: Contrast the two pages, remarking on the differences in clarity. On the first two pages the trees and the distant landscape are still hidden in the fog, then on pages 18 and 19 the trees, the ground, the children, and the distant islands come into sharp focus. The reader can almost feel the freshness and sparkle of the morning.

   • Pages 20–25: These pages continue to reflect the contrasts of soft, muted colors and deep, vibrant hues. Point out that the sailing picture almost looks stormy, with the whitecaps on the waves, the shape of the sail filled with wind, and the clouds on the horizon. The swimming illustrations are bright and colorful, whereas the castle-building pages return to the hazy softness of pastels.

   • Pages 26–29: Show the students how the nighttime seems close and protective on the first two pages and vast and awesome on the next pages. The reflections of the stars in the water are especially noteworthy.

   • Pages 30–35: Point out how the sky changes reinforce the text descriptions of the waning season. Reread the first paragraph on page 30 and the last paragraph on page 32.

   • Pages 36–43: Ask the students what clues in the illustrations tell them of the approaching storm. (gathering supplies, the flat stillness of the water, the gulls solemnly facing in one direction, the dark colors of the sky mirrored in the darkness of the water, and the grays and blacks woven through the pages)

   • Pages 44–49: Ask the students how the illustrations convey the strength and fury of the storm. (the taut line anchoring the boat, the bent pine tree, the whoosh of movement to the right on each of the pages, the circle of light capturing the family on the couch)

   • Pages 50–57: Have students note carefully the aftermath of the storm in the slow appearance of the moon and its light, the calming of the waters, the uprooted and broken trees, and the girls' discovery of the Indian shell heap.

- Pages 58–63: Show the students how the colors stand out on each of the pages: the bright yellow of the sunflowers, the soft apricot of the sky, and the wonderful sunset of orange hues streaming onto the water.

3. Ask two student volunteers to search the poster for the year the story won. (Searching the poster helps students become familiar with the many different titles selected for the award.)

Ask students to think about how Mr. McCloskey illustrated the magic of summers in Maine, then return in their own imaginations to the summer experiences that are memorable for them. As they immerse themselves in these mental pictures, have them begin to picture the scenes they will draw about these summer "times of wonder." Distribute the drawing paper and allow them to use the illustrating medium that best fits their experiences. When students are finished, have them select display spots on the wall or the clothesline, then plan how they will present their pictures to the class. Tour the line of pictures and have each student share a few words about the picture and the feelings it evokes. (*Visual/Spatial Intelligence*)

➤ Activity Plan 2: Summer Poems—Free Verse

Materials

Scrabble Creek by Patricia Wittmann (New York: Macmillan, 1993)
Transparency of figure 10.1, Scrabble Creek Poem

Engage

Write these words on the board: *Free Verse*. Invite student comments and connections about free verse. (What is it? How is it written?) (*Verbal/Linguistic Intelligence*)

Elaborate

Address the students as follows:

McCloskey's book, *Time of Wonder*, is like one long free verse poem celebrating the wonders of a summer vacation in Maine. We will be writing our own free verse poems about the summer experiences we illustrated in the beginning lesson. To begin to think about our writing, let's start with charades and dramatize behaviors/ activities we love or enjoy in one of these categories: places, activities, foods, or sports.

Scrabble Creek

On a warm summer evening
arriving at last,
The crackle of the campfire
scaring away the night noises,
The laughter from Sam's dumb jokes,
Shadows as black as crows
The lantern's yellow circle of light at
the bunkhouse,
The flare of suddenly roasting
marshmallows,
Building a fairy house in the shadowy
woods,
Sitting on my favorite rock,
Imagining I am Princess Mossy Rock,
Snuggling into my old, soft sleeping bag,
I'm a big kid now!

➤ Figure 10.1. Scrabble Creek Poem

Invite students to think of ideas, announce their categories, and dramatize behaviors that would make the audience guess the ideas. Foods (ice cream, pizza, sodas), sports (football, soccer, karate, biking), and amusement park rides are popular choices; other ideas include shopping trips to the mall, playing a musical instrument, talking on the telephone, playing video games, and watching television. (*Bodily/Kinesthetic Intelligence*)

Explore

Read *Scrabble Creek*, the story of a special summer camping trip. Ask the students why the camping trip is memorable. (the first splash in the creek, the swimming hole, campfires and roasting marshmallows, fairy houses in the woods, snuggling down deep into a sleeping bag, being a big kid)

Prewriting

The students should think about the summer experiences described in *Time of Wonder* and *Scrabble Creek* as they imagine the words for their own memorable summer experiences. Guide their brainstorming with the following steps (figure 10.2 shows a sample prewrite brainstorming page):

1. Our first list of words will focus on action words about the topics. Think of the actions described by Mr. McCloskey. Slowly review the book, and list the actions that are described: a million splashing raindrops, the lifting fog, sailing among the islands, swimming and diving on the point, stretching out in the sun, building sand castles, rowing for home, gazing at stars, weathering a hurricane, combing the beach for shells, packing for home.

   What actions are described in *Scrabble Creek?* (arriving at Scrabble Creek, jumping out of the car, splashing in the creek and skipping rocks, wading, swimming, sunning, roasting and eating marshmallows, building fairy houses, playing cards, walking through the wet grass to the bunkhouse)

   What actions happen in your favorite summer experience? (Give students time to think of many ideas and circulate and encourage collaboration and discussion.)

2. Draw lines across your paper to indicate new ideas, then begin the second list of words and phrases. As you imagine yourself reliving the experience, what color/sight words and phrases would describe what you see?

   Think about McCloskey's descriptions. Browse the book and list the ideas that are remembered: clouds peeping over Camden Hills, thirty miles away across the bay, ghostlike trees in the early morning fog, sparkling blue waters, a mother seal nursing her baby, hundreds of stars in the night sky, low tide and high tide, gulls sitting solemnly, preparing for the storm, the bright moonlight, the frosty coating of salt on the windows, snow-white clam shells, sunflower faces lifting to the sun.

   What colors and sights are remembered in *Scrabble Creek?* (the sand path, shadows black as crows, a small and cozy trailer, the yellow circle of light)

   What colors and sights do you see in your summer experiences? (Again, give students time to think of many ideas and circulate and encourage collaboration and discussion.)

Prewrite Brainstorming: Summer in Maine

Action words and phrases:

a million splashing raindrops, the lifting fog, sailing among the islands, swimming and diving on the point, stretching out in the sun, building sand castles, rowing for home, gazing at stars, weathering a hurricane, combing the beach for shells, packing for home

Color/sights words and phrases:

clouds peeping over the Camden Hills, thirty miles away across the bay, ghost-like trees in the early morning fog, sparkling bue waters, a mother seal nursing her baby, hundreds of stars in the night sky, low tide and high tide, gulls sitting solemnly, preparing for the storm, the bright moonlight, the frosty coating of salt on the windows, snow-white clam shells, sunflower faces lifting to the sun

Sound words and phrases:

the snorting sound of a family of porpoises, a ripple and splash along the shore, giggling and laughing gulls and cormorants, buzzing bees, an owl asking a question and a heron croaking an answer, the tolling bell-buoy off Spectacle Island, the roar of the hurricane, the scream of the wind, Mother reading a story, the sounds of leave-taking, "all aboard"

Feeling word and phrases:

the foggy morning feeling of isolation, the sudden joy of the sun burning the fog away, the happy contentment of a day swimming on the point and sailing among the islands, the quiet satisfaction of night-time star-gazing, the alert watchfulness in the approaching storm, the feeling that you are glad to be home, safe with your family, the wonder of familiar paths changed by the storm, the sadness of leave-taking until another summer

➤ Figure 10.2. Prewrite: Summer Experiences

3. Draw lines across your paper to indicate new ideas, then begin the third list of words and phrases. As you imagine yourself enjoying the summer experience again, what sounds do you recall?

McCloskey's story really brings alive the sounds of the islands—the snorting sound of a family of porpoises, a ripple and splash along the shore, giggling and laughing gulls and cormorants, buzzing bees, an owl asking a question and a heron croaking an answer, the tolling bell buoy off Spectacle Island, the roar of the hurricane, the scream of the wind, Mother reading a story, the sounds of leave-taking, "all aboard."

What sounds are used in *Scrabble Creek*? (plip, plip, plip, plop of skipping rocks; sploosh of Dad pretending to be a whale; Sam's dumb jokes; ka-wok of frogs croaking; night noises) What sounds do you hear in your summer experiences?

4. The words in our final list describe feelings and emotions associated with our favorite summer experiences. From *Time of Wonder*, we gather these ideas—the foggy morning feeling of isolation, the sudden joy of the sun burning the fog away, the happy contentment of a day swimming on the point and sailing among the islands, the quiet satisfaction of nighttime stargazing, the alert watchfulness in the approaching storm, the feeling that you are glad to be home, safe with your family, the wonder of familiar paths changed by the storm, the sadness of leave-taking until another summer.

What feelings and emotions are remembered in *Scrabble Creek*? (the joy of arrival, the fun of revisiting favorite places, the feeling of well-being from dinner in the outdoors, feeling afraid of the sounds in the night, contentment in creating fairy houses with Alice, pride in being one of the big kids now)

What feelings and emotions do you associate with your summer experiences?

Connect

Have students complete the rough drafting step of the writing process. Show the transparency of the poem about Scrabble Creek (see figure 10.1) and list the guidelines for writing the free verse poems. The poems should be eight lines in length and include two action ideas, two sound words and phrases, three sight descriptions, and one feeling expression (see figure 10.3).

➤ Figure 10.3. Free Verse Poem Guidelines

Free Verse Poems

Eight lines in length

Include:
Two action ideas
Two sound words and phrases
Three sight descriptions
One feeling expression

Students will often ask if they can write longer poems, but it is better to encourage them to carefully craft these eight lines and work at identifying the essence of the summer experiences and expressing it in this short format. By concentrating on these eight lines, students can focus on selecting powerful verbs and adjectives and building vivid mental pictures of the summer experiences. Before beginning first drafts, encourage students to once again imagine themselves in the midst of the experiences they are describing, then use the prewrite brainstorming ideas and begin to craft the poems. Some students will immediately know the shapes of their poems, others will struggle to begin. A strategy that can help is to ask the student to circle the words and phrases that evoke the most connections to the summer experience, then select the most meaningful phrase as a beginning. Circulate as students work, providing encouragement and feedback; "what" questions help students elaborate on ideas and develop the images. (What kind of horse? What color was the sky? What words would describe that actual sound?)

➤ Activity Plan 3: Revising Summer Poems—Adding Details

Materials

Scrap paper
Pencils

Engage

Ask the students to solve this riddle: What am I?

- I am a bright splash of red, covered with yellow and blue stripes and dots,

- Floating lazily above the treetops in the cloudless, blue sky.

- My string is clasped tightly in the small child's hand, dark hair gleaming in the noonday sun.

What am I? (a kite or a balloon)

Discuss what details helped students picture the scene.
Then try another example:

- The nooks and crannies of the barn are my favorite hiding places.

- Darting and running, faster than the blink of an eye, I carry grains and seeds and maybe a pea or two to my snug home in the hay.

- With my small pointed ears standing alert, my long, narrow tail,

- twitching gently, and my tiny whiskers quivering fearfully.

- I await my enemy—the cat.

What am I? (Mouse)
Discuss which details confirm the answer.

Elaborate

Write some descriptive phrases on the board to remind students of the kinds of phrases and clues they should develop about their mystery objects/choices. Talk about the strategy of building pictures in the mind. Descriptive words and phrases should help students create mental photographs of the mystery objects/choices. Circulate as students are writing clues and encourage them to select interesting words; for example, if the object is fast, ask the student what a more interesting synonym for *fast* would be, and how we might know more precisely how swift. (The student should use a simile.) Remind students to really bring us into the scene where we are observing the mystery object. (*Verbal/Linguistic Intelligence*)

Explore

Have students share their mystery object clues, and let the class guess the objects. Encourage them to read slowly so the rest of the class has an opportunity to build mental pictures. Remark on well-written clues (in terms of the pictures they build).

Connect

Remind students of the power of the "what" question when they are adding details and thinking about descriptions to help the reader be part of the scene: What colors? What feelings are you experiencing? What kind of dog? Have students work with partners and use the mystery object experience and "what" question strategy to revise their summer experience poems by adding details. One partner should share his or her poem, and the other partner should list a variety of "what" questions that come to mind; they should then repeat the process with the other student's poem. Then students can select the "what" questions they want to answer to add detail to their poems. (*Interpersonal and Verbal/Linguistic Intelligences*)

➤ Activity Plan 4: Revising Summer Poems— Selecting Powerful Words

Materials

Charade slips (activity sheet 10.1)
Thesaurus dictionaries (One per student is the ideal, but you can still facilitate this revision step if student partners share dictionaries.)

crunch	stride
nibble	march
devour	tiptoe
swallow	amble
gulp	stroll
dine	shuffle
chew	stomp
chomp	swagger

➤Activity Sheet 10.1. Synonym Charade Slips

Engage

Write *Eat* and *Walk* on the board and have students use charades to identify more interesting synonyms for these words. (See activity sheet 10.1 for suggested words.) Using activity sheet 10.1, cut apart the synonyms, fold them, and place them in a container. Invite student volunteers to draw synonym slips from the container and act out the word on it while the rest of the class guesses. After a synonym has been dramatized and guessed by the class, record it on the board in the appropriate list. After all the words have been listed on the board, review them and emphasize how much more descriptive than the original words some of the synonyms are. (*Bodily/Kinesthetic Intelligence*)

Elaborate

Model using the thesaurus dictionary. Remind students that the thesaurus is in alphabetical order just like a regular dictionary. Invite them to find some words and list the synonyms that are found. (Easy words to use are *small, smile, friendly,* and *courage.*)

Explore

Have students circle words in their poems that could be improved, then use the thesaurus dictionaries to make revisions. Encourage collaboration and discussion with peers; students may also need dictionaries to confirm the appropriateness of their substitutions. Circulate as students are working and use questioning and comments about the mental pictures their words bring up to help them evaluate the effectiveness of their choices. (*Verbal/Linguistic Intelligence*)

Connect

If students have access to computers, schedule computer lab time and have them type the poems (otherwise print or write the poems in cursive). Poems should be centered on the page; before they print the poems, have students conference with peers to check spelling, punctuation, capitalization, and spacing. Attach the poems to the left or right of the summer illustrations drawn during the first lesson, Sharing the Story. (See figure 10.4 for an example.)

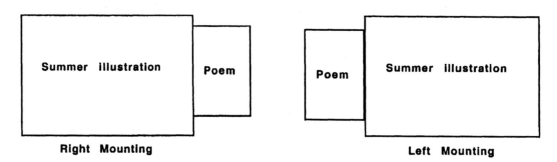

➤Figure 10.4. Publishing the Poems

➤Activity Plan 5: Fall Poems—Two-Word Poems

Materials

Look What I Did with a Leaf by Morteza E. Sohi (New York: Walker, 1993)
Leaves collected by students
Time of Wonder by Robert McCloskey
Paper towels (for drying and pressing leaves)
Glue
Transparency of figure 10.5
Transparency and multiple copies (one per student) of activity sheet 10.2
Thesaurus dictionaries

Engage

Show the leaves you have gathered and share the book *Look What I Did with a Leaf.* Explain to students that they will be illustrating their fall poems with leaf pictures and encourage them to begin gathering a selection of leaves for drying. (*Visual/Spatial Intelligence*)

To dry and press the leaves, lay a paper towel on a flat surface and use a marker to print a student's name, then arrange the student's leaves on the paper towel. Place a second paper towel on top of the leaves, and repeat the process with other students' leaves until several layers are formed. Stack encyclopedias or other heavy books on top of the leaf layers and let the leaves dry for three or four days.

Return briefly to *Time of Wonder* in search of autumn references or images:

- Pages 30–31 have effective description and illustration.

- Page 32 begins the storm sequence, and we associate hurricanes with the season of fall.

- Page 60 mentions the return to school, an annual autumn event.

Elaborate

Display the transparency of the two-word poems listed in figure 10.5 so students can see the format of the poems. Share the poems.

Explore

Model the process of writing the two-word poem.

Autumn

Crimson leaves,
rustling rhythms
on a
foggy dawn;
scurrying squirrels'
acorn harvest,
winter preparation;
white woodsmoke
mingling through
bare branches;
crisp, crunchy
apple banquet
shared by
laughing, pink-cheeked
beaming children.

Quilt

Sky-blue quilt,
red stars,
yellow stripes
named comforter,
warming bodies,
brightening bedrooms,
giving security,
drying tears,
keeping secrets,
catching crumbs,
sharing problems,
experiencing laughter!

Kite

Bright cerulean,
dazzling yellow,
glittering emerald,
long tailed
dragon kite,
dipping, swaying,
in the
twilight sky;
swiftly flying,
soaring smoothly,
over the distant treetops.

➤ Figure 10.5. Two-Word Poems

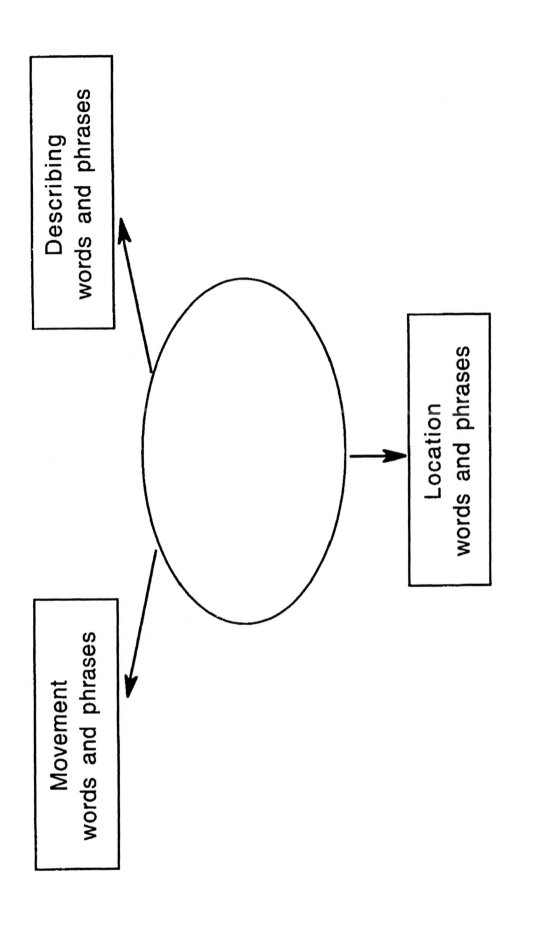

Describing
words and phrases

Location
words and phrases

Movement
words and phrases

▶ Activity Sheet 10.2. Prewrite Brainstorming: Two-Word Poems

Prewrite Brainstorming

Pick a topic familiar to the students (balloon, cat, soccer ball, automobile) and use the transparency of activity sheet 10.2 to brainstorm words and phrases about the topic. Have students work with partners to begin thinking of ideas (this strategy encourages broader participation), then create a class web of ideas. Figure 10.6 lists prewriting brainstorming ideas for a poem about a cat.

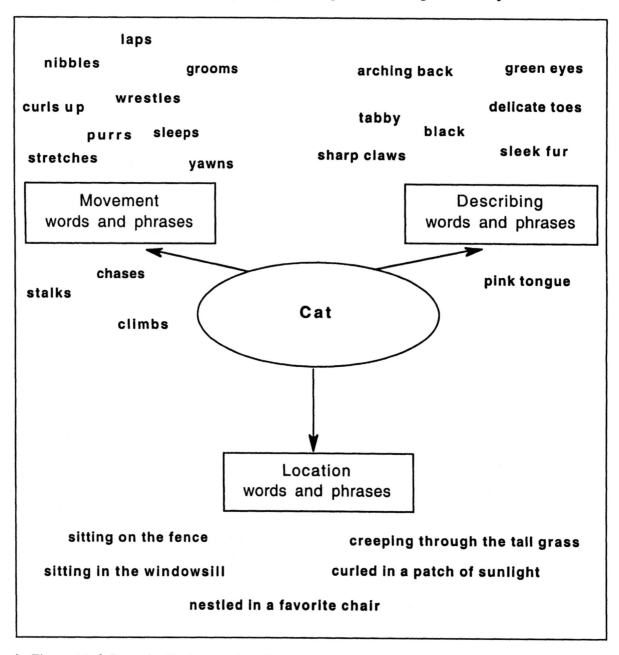

➤ Figure 10.6. Prewrite Brainstorming: Cat

Rough Drafting

Use the words and phrases in the prewrite brainstorming to write the two-word poem. Remind students that each line should form a complete picture. (Occasionally, for the sense of the poem, a line may be a bridge to the complete idea; you will notice this in the third line of the "Autumn" poem and in the seventh and eleventh lines of the "Kite" poem in figure 10.5. Encourage students to limit the use of bridge lines.) See figure 10.7 for a two-word poem, written from the brainstorming, about a cat. (*Verbal/Linguistic and Interpersonal Intelligences*)

Cat

Black cat
curled-in sunlight,
yawns, stretches,
shows claws,
gets up, stands
stiff legs,
yawns more,
sharp teeth,
pink tongue,
arching back,
delicate toes
slowly climbs
garden fence.

➤ Figure 10.7. Cat Poem

Cat

Chestnut cat
curled-in sunlight,
yawns, stretches,
uncloaks claws,
rises, stands
stiff legs,
yawns more,
sharp teeth,
pink tongue,
arching back,
delicate toes
climbs leisurely
over the
garden fence.

➤ Figure 10.8. Revised Cat Poem

Revising

Help students use the thesaurus dictionaries to improve the "class-created" poem. Circle words that could be improved: *black, shows, gets up,* and *slowly.* Use the thesaurus dictionaries to select some possibilities for *black* (*tawny, chestnut,* and *russet*); read the poem and see which color word fits best. Repeat the process with the other words. For example, *uncloaks* could replace *shows; rises* could be a substitute for *gets up;* and *leisurely* would be more interesting than *slowly.* See figure 10.8 for the revised poem.

Publishing

Help students plan an illustration for the poem the class has created. Ask them how they would use leaves in the illustration. (long, narrow, dark green leaves for the pickets of the garden fence and a selection of small, dark red or deep brown leaves to make the cat) (*Visual/Spatial Intelligence*)

Connect

To help students select topics for their two-word fall poems, brainstorm a class list of ideas and images associated with autumn (figure 10.9 presents some ideas). Then have students use the prewrite brainstorming forms (see activity sheet 10.2) to gather words and phrases for their poems. After they write their rough drafts, encourage students to conference with peers to circle words that could be enhanced by using the thesaurus dictionaries. (*Verbal/Linguistic and Interpersonal Intelligences*)

Autumn Events **pumpkins** **red, gold, and orange leaves** **apples** **migrating birds** **raking leaves** **harvesting crops** **squirrels and chipmunks** **gathering food** **frosty mornings** **crisp, cool days**

➤ Figure 10.9. Autumn Events

When publishing, students should plan their leaf illustrations and decide the best placement of the poems. If students have access to computers, schedule computer lab time for them to type the poems. They should use the return key and the space bar to position poems according to the planning illustration. Before they print the poems, have students conference with peers to check spelling, punctuation, capitalization, and spacing. Remove the leaves from the drying stack and have students use glue to paste leaves into the illustrations they have planned. Be careful not to stack the finished pages until the glue has thoroughly dried (usually overnight is long enough). (*Visual/Spatial Intelligence*)

➤ Activity Plan 6: Winter Poems—Haiku

Materials

Red Dragonfly on My Shoulder translated by Sylvia Cassedy and Kunihiro Suetake
  (New York: Harper, 1992)
Time of Wonder by Robert McCloskey
Transparency of the haiku poem rules (figure 10.10)

Engage

Introduce haiku poetry by sharing poems from *Red Dragonfly on My Shoulder*. Don't discuss the poems, just let students quietly absorb the images and the words. Pause as you turn each page to let students closely examine the illustrations before they hear the words. (*Visual/Spatial and Verbal/Linguistic Intelligences*)

Elaborate

Share this information: Haiku originated in Japan. It is simple, rich, expressive verse that captures and describes a moment in nature. The poem gives the essentials and relies on the imagination of the reader to expand the image and supply the details.

Several of the illustrations in *Time of Wonder* would spark wonderful haiku poems:

- Pages 6–7: Clouds over island waters, cast creeping shadows, approaching rainstorm.

- Pages 14–15: On foggy mornings, the forest is so quiet, sounds of growing ferns.

- Pages 28–29: Quiet of the night, hundreds of stars glimmering, now I'm safely home.

- Pages 38–39: On rocky ledges, seabirds perch in solemn rows, no time for cackling.

- Pages 52–53: In the bright moonlight, the wind quiets, lessening the crashing of the waves.

Continue to develop the students' awareness of the haiku format. Read one of the poems from figure 10.11. Let students think about the images for a moment, then ask them to draw pictures of what they see. This helps them visualize the important parts of a haiku poem: the subject, the location of the subject, and the action taking place. Invite students to share their pictures, then discuss the poem to identify the season, the subject, the location, and the action taking place. Repeat this process with one or two of the other haiku poems. (*Visual/Spatial Intelligence*)

Haiku Poetry

1. They capture and describe scenes in nature.

In the evening sun,
Waves break on the rocky shore,
Shadows of seagulls.

Leaves of red and orange
Rustle in the harvest wind,
Scampering chipmunks.

2. They use descriptive language to hint at the season of the poem. They do not use the words: autumn, fall, winter, spring, summer.

A foggy morning,
Sandpipers run, avoiding
The water's edge.

Wandering snowflakes,
A cardinal perches in
The snow-covered pine.

3. They do not repeat words.

4. They follow this format:

> **Line 1:   5 syllables**
> **Line 2:   7 syllables**
> **Line 3:   5 syllables**

Evening on the pond,
Canada geese glide slowly
Through paths of sunlight.

Peaceful forest walk
Among towering cedars,
A dogwood blossoms.

5. They:

> **Tell what the subject is (only one).**
> **Tell where the subject is.**
> **Tell what action is taking place (only one action).**

Lazy afternoon,
Red-winged blackbird holds fast and
Sways on the cattail.

Fragrance of lilacs,
I contemplate small footprints
In the dewy yard.

➤ Figure 10.10. Haiku Poem Rules

Explore

As a prewrite brainstorming activity, use the transparency (figure 10.10) to review the haiku poem rules.

Short days, longer nights, the maple's leaves turn to gold in the brisk north wind.	Ghostly bare-limbed trees, in cold moonlight I listen, the call of the owl.
Season: Autumn Subject: The maple's leaves Location: In the north wind Action: Turn to gold	Season: Winter Subject: A person Location: Cold moonlight Action: Listening for an owl
Radiant moonlight, shadows of forsythia move on my window.	Mornings at the farm, distant sounds carry across the terraced wheat fields.
Season: Spring Subject: Forsythia shadows Location: On the window Action: Flickering and moving	Season: Summer Subject: Distant sounds Location: Across the fields Action: Seem very close

➤**Figure 10.11. Haiku Poems**

1. *They capture and describe scenes in nature.* Have students listen to the two examples and describe the settings in nature they visualize.

2. *They use descriptive language to hint at the season of the poem. They do not use the words: autumn, fall, winter, spring, summer.* Ask students what seasons come to mind when they hear these two examples.

3. *They do not repeat words.* Because so few syllables are used in the haiku poem format, word choices are particularly important.

4. *They follow this format:*

    - Line 1: Five syllables

    - Line 2: Seven syllables

    - Line 3: Five syllables

To reinforce the syllable format, have students clap or tap the syllables in the two examples.

5. They:

- Tell what the subject is (only one).

- Tell where the subject is.

- Tell what action is taking place (only one action).

As students listen to the examples, have them identify the three components.

Because the haiku poems the students will write will celebrate winter experiences and memories, help the students brainstorm words and phrases that indicate winter. Have students work with partners to begin making their lists, then create a class idea bank of words and phrases about winter. If students are stumped for ideas you might suggest words or phrases such as the following: frost sparkling on windows, hibernating animals, howling blizzard, icicles hanging from the eaves, drifting snowflakes, cold, silver days, sleigh bells, skies filled with cold-white crystals, chill, biting wind, ground thick with slush and sleet, snowy footsteps, frozen ribbon of water, the tracks of the snowshoe hare, a ring of nibbled bark, the weasel's white fur, polar bears slip and slide on the ice, silently, softly comes the snow. (*Interpersonal Intelligence*)

Keep the bank of winter words and phrases visible to students, and as another step in prewrite brainstorming, have students imagine and sketch winter scenes. Be sure they save these rough sketches; they will be used at the publishing stage as the idea banks for the watercolor paintings. (*Visual/Spatial Intelligence*)

Connect

Once again, display the transparency of the rules for writing haiku poems (figure 10.10) and have students write rough drafts about the scenes they have illustrated.

If students need some ideas, following are some examples from classes that have used this activity:

1. One student illustrated a variety of trees: some were pines and some were deciduous with bare, snow-laden branches. Snow filled the foreground of the picture, and slightly buried in the snow to the left of the picture was a single bright red mitten. Following is the haiku poem that accompanied the picture:

> Laughter of children,
> a bright red mitten lies lost
> in the snowy woods.

When discussing the poem, the student shared that he loved the snowy woods behind his house and had imagined how the red mitten came to be left behind. He felt it wasn't important to actually see the children in the picture, and that's why he created the phrase "laughter of children," to remind readers of their lingering echo and to give a possible explanation for the mitten being there.

2. Another student drew a picture of a frost-covered window and wrote this poem:

> I awaken to
> frost sparkling on the window,
> cloudless sky, sunshine.

3. A third student drew a snow-covered meadow with several small trees and some sparsely placed grasses; a trail of footprints wandered through the meadow. This is what she wrote about the scene:

> A snowshoe hare roams
> the meadow, looking for food,
> rings of nibbled bark.

➤ Activity Plan 7: Haiku Poems— Revising and Publishing

Materials

Thesaurus dictionaries
Watercolor pigments (available from the art teacher or an art supply store)
Brushes (available from the art teacher or an art supply store)

Engage

Invite students to share their haiku poem rough drafts.

Elaborate

To help students revise their poems, select one of the poems and make a sketch of the picture you see. As you draw, explain the setting, subject, and action you picture, then identify how you know the poem describes a winter scene. Invite questions from the student whose poem you are illustrating. For example, the student who wrote:

laughter of children,
a bright red mitten lies lost
in the snowy woods

might ask how you picture the depth of the snow and what kinds of trees you see. Other questions might be: What color is the sky? Is the snow smooth and unmarked or filled with footprints? The questions help students compare the mental picture they intended with the interpretation seen by you as you drew and talked about the poem. This sharing and discussion help the partner think about changes that would make the poem images more vivid and clearly defined. (*Visual/Spatial and Verbal/ Linguistic Intelligences*)

A second revision strategy is to check the syllable count. Tap or clap the syllables in each line to see that they follow the five-seven-five syllable pattern.

Explore

Have students exchange poems with partners, read the poems, and draw pictures of the images they see. As they share their impressions (pictures) with their partners and describe what they have drawn, encourage them to identify the seasonal references, the settings, the subjects, and the actions, and invite questions and discussion. This experience (seeing what a partner drew after reading the poem and discussing the poems) will help students see their poems with fresh eyes and make word improvements to build stronger images. After they make word improvements, have students complete syllable pattern checks. (*Interpersonal and Visual/Spatial Intelligences*)

Connect

Have students use their prewrite rough sketches to complete watercolor paintings that illustrate their winter haiku poems. If students have access to computers, schedule computer lab time for them to type up the poems. Before they print the poems, have students conference with peers to check spelling, punctuation, capitalization, and spacing. They should then print the poems, trim around the poems to create interesting shapes, and paste them in the watercolor scenes. For example, one student decided that the poem and its surrounding shape would become a cloud in his painting; another student printed the poem so it could become part of a tall tree trunk and used the watercolor paints to add texture and color. Be careful not to stack the finished pages until the watercolors have thoroughly dried (overnight is usually long enough). (*Visual/Spatial Intelligence*)

➤ Activity Plan 8: Spring Poems—Five Ws Poetry

Materials

Transparency of figure 10.12
Transparency of figure 10.13
Time of Wonder by Robert McCloskey
Transparency of figure 10.14

Thesaurus dictionaries
Drawing paper
Variety of materials for creating collages (wallpaper samples, construction paper, tissue
    paper, wrapping paper)
Scissors
Glue

Engage

Share the poems in figure 10.12, then display the transparency and list the five Ws on
the board (Who? What? Where? When? Why?); invite students to participate in matching the five
Ws to the lines of the first poem:

- Who is the subject of the poem? (John)

- What is the subject doing? (roller blading)

- Where is the subject? (along the river path)

- When does this take place? (in the warm sunshine)

- Why? (celebrating the freedom of a spring day)

Repeat the process with the other poems on the transparency.

Elaborate

Turn to pages 44 and 45 in *Time of Wonder* and have students imagine themselves in the
midst of this storm. Display the transparency of the five Ws questions (figure 10.13), and compose a class
poem based on the scene in the book. Following is an example. (*Visual/Spatial and Verbal/Linguistic
Intelligences*)

Line one, Who: a small boat
Line two, What: rises and falls in the sharp, choppy waves,
Line three, Where: pulling at its anchor in the cove.
Line four, When: nighttime storm
Line five, Why: whips the water.

Explore

Prewriting

To help students select topics for their five Ws spring poems, brainstorm a class list of
ideas and images associated with spring (figure 10.14 presents some ideas).

John
loves to roller blade
along the river path
in the warm sunshine,
celebrating the freedom of a spring day.

The baby birds
cheep loudly
from their safe nest in the pine.
It's sunset,
and they are waiting hungrily for tasty
insects.

A black and green caterpillar
slowly crawled
through the garden seedlings
in the early morning dew,
searching for a new leaf.

➤ Figure 10.12. Five Ws Poems

---

5 Ws Questions

Who is the subject?

What is the subject doing?   What is the action?

Where is the subject?

When does the action happen?

Why is it happening?

➤ Figure 10.13. Five Ws Questions

Spring Events

**ducklings, goslings, lambs,
or other baby animals
tulips, daffodils,
tree buds
apple blossoms
tadpoles
melting snow
earthworms
robins
Easter eggs
spring storms
butterflies**

➤ Figure 10.14. Spring Events

Have students write the five Ws on lined paper, leaving several spaces between each line (see figure 10.15).

```
┌─────────────────────────────┐
│        Topic:               │
│                             │
│ Who?                        │
│                             │
│ What?                       │
│                             │
│ Where?                      │
│                             │
│ When?                       │
│                             │
│ Why?                        │
└─────────────────────────────┘
```

➤ **Figure 10.15. Five Ws Brainstorming**

Display the transparency of figure 10.13 (the five Ws questions). Encourage students to select ideas from the spring topics list and have them brainstorm responses.

Rough Drafting

Use the transparency of figure 10.16 to review the guidelines for writing a five Ws poem. Tell students to imagine themselves in the spring scenes they are describing, use their prewriting brainstorming words and phrases, and begin to write first drafts.

Revising

Select a line from one of the poems shared at the beginning of the lesson or from the poem created by the class and model using the thesaurus to improve word choices. For example:

> The baby birds
> cheep loudly
> from their safe nest in the pine.
> It's sunset,
> and they are waiting hungrily for tasty
> insects.

Students searched the thesaurus for improvements to these words: *cheep, loudly, safe, sunset, waiting,* and *tasty. Loudly* was changed to *noisily; safe* was replaced by *secluded; sunset* became *dusk;* and *tasty* was changed to *delicious.* No substitutes were made for *cheep* and *waiting.* Figure 10.17 shows the revised poem.

Have students work with thesaurus dictionaries to make improvements to their first drafts. Encourage discussion and collaboration.

Guidelines for the 5 Ws Poem

Line 1 names the subject of your poem.

Line 2 describes actions of the subject. It tells what the subject is doing.

Line 3 tells the setting and shows where the action is taking place.

Line 4 adds information to the setting and describes the "time" of the poem.

Line 5 explains why this action is occurring.

➤ Figure 10.16. Guidelines for Writing a Five Ws Poem

The baby birds
cheep noisely
from their secluded nest in the pine.
It's dusk,
and they are waiting hungrily for
delicious insects.

➤ Figure 10.17. Revised Five Ws Poem

Connect

Publishing

Torn-paper collage illustrations make very effective illustrations for the poems. Gather a variety of materials (wallpaper samples, construction paper, tissue paper, wrapping paper), scissors, and glue and have students plan collage illustrations to accompany their spring five Ws poems. For example, if a student were illustrating the poem about John roller blading along the river path, he or she could place the poem on the upper left side of the paper (see figure 10.18). (*Visual/Spatial and Verbal/Linguistic Intelligences*)

The student could then fill the paper above and around the poem with torn pieces of blue construction paper in a variety of shades of blue to create the sky. Near the bottom of the paper he or she could create a path from gray and black tissue paper sprinkled with grit. Strips of tissue paper in white, blue, and yellow could be layered slightly above the path to create the water of the river. The colors from the tissue paper strips would bleed into each other, creating an interesting water effect. To emphasize the separation of path and water, the student could add delicately fringed pieces of green paper for wetlands grasses. Final touches could include a gray construction paper boulder, wispy cattails, and the figure of John skating along the path. (*Visual/Spatial Intelligence*)

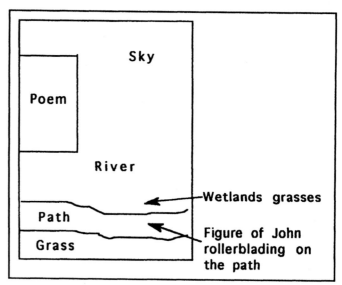

➤ Figure 10.18. Torn-Paper Collage Illustration

If students have access to computers, schedule computer lab time for them to type the poems. Before they print the poems, have students conference with peers to check spelling, punctuation, capitalization, and spacing.

11 Tuesday

Written by David Wiesner
Illustrated by David Wiesner
New York: Clarion Books, 1991

Summary

➤ On Tuesday around eight in the evening frogs rose on their lily pads, floated through the air, and explored the nearby houses while the inhabitants slept. They alarmed a late-night snacker, slipped quietly by a sleeping late-night television watcher, excited a neighbor dog, and eventually returned to their homes in the pond, leaving the detective to puzzle over the discarded lily pads found in the street the next day.

Award Year

➤ 1992

Art Information

➤ Illustrated using watercolors.

Curriculum Connections

➤ Mysteries

➤Activity Plan 1: Sharing the Story

Materials

Green construction paper lily pads
Caldecott Award poster
Watercolor paint (available at art supply stores)
Paintbrush
Small cup of water
Drawing paper
Illustrating materials (pencils, watercolors, markers, crayons)

Engage

Before students enter the room, scatter the construction paper lily pads throughout the room. Speculate with students about their presence; be dramatic and explain what happened. (You entered the room this morning and found them.) Ask the students: Why are they here? What do they mean? What is this mystery? I wonder if it has anything to do with this story. (*Verbal/Linguistic Intelligence*)

Elaborate

Share the story.

Explore

Discuss the story. Ask the students: What caused the frogs to fly from the pond? (Invite speculation.) Do you suppose it was the full moon? (Remind students that like the idea that there is a man's face in the moon or that the moon is made of green cheese, there is also the idea that the full moon causes odd behaviors.) What conclusions might the detective make? What will the pigs do? How will the pattern continue? What happens next? Why are mysteries so fascinating? What are mysteries that puzzle you?

Connect

Share the Caldecott Award information:

1. As students examine the cover of the book, ask them what special thing they notice. (gold medal) Ask them what the name of the medal is. (Caldecott Award Medal) Ask them why it has been placed on this book. (Some answers may be: The illustrations are special, well done, particularly interesting, exciting, and/or unusual.)

2. Discuss the art techniques used in creating the pictures. Browse the pictures and comment on Mr. Wiesner's ability to capture the look of full-moon nights; it's nighttime but the light of the full moon brings a clarity to the objects of the night and seems to make them easier to see.

> Watercolors are the medium used to create the illustrations, and these illustrations seem to have a more concentrated application of the paint. [Show the difference between application of watercolors when only a little water is used and when a lot of water is used.] The more water is used, the more transparent the color becomes.

3. Ask two student volunteers to search the poster for the year the story won. (Searching the poster helps students become familiar with the many different titles selected for the award.)

Have students work with partners to illustrate new pages for the book to show how the pattern might continue (birds swimming in the pond, sheep climbing trees, cats flying). Each partnership will produce three pages (*Visual/Spatial and Interpersonal Intelligences*):

- Page 1 will show the words, "Next Tuesday," 7:58 P.M.

- Page 2 will display the first illustration, which identifies the setting.

- Page 3 will illustrate what is happening in the setting.

➤ Activity Plan 2: What Is Your Alias?

Materials

> *Ed Emberley's Great Thumbprint Drawing Book* (Boston: Little, Brown, 1977)
> Ink pads (two or three of them)
> Paper towel sheets (for cleanup)
> Alias activity sheets (activity sheet 11.1; one per student)
> Small sheets of white construction paper (5 x 5 inch; one per student)
> Magnifying glasses (optional)

Engage

Pass among the students and have them make thumbprints using the ink pads. Give them time to compare their thumbprints with other students and note similarities and differences. (*Visual/Spatial and Logical/Mathematical Intelligences*)

What is your alias?
Name:
Alias(es):
Occupation:
D.O.B.

Height:	Build:
Hair:	Eyes:

Habits:	
Left Hand Thumbprint:	Right Hand Thumbprint:

➤Activity Sheet 11.1. Alias Worksheet

Elaborate

Fingerprints are unique to each person, and because they are, they have become an important identification method in crime detection and solving mysteries. We leave fingerprints on any smooth objects we touch—the chair, the table, our notebooks—and detectives use these recovered fingerprints to match a suspect to the scene of a mystery. The lab detectives sprinkle black powder at the scene of the mystery, then use special papers to lift the prints. They closely compare the ridges and swirls of these prints to the prints of the suspects and then solve the mystery.

Explore

Use Ed Emberley's book to show students how to make drawings from thumbprints, then let students use the small sheets of construction paper, make thumbprints, and turn the thumbprints into drawings.

Have students complete the alias sheet (activity sheet 11.1). Alias sheets are information sheets completed by detectives and police officers that give information about suspects: their nicknames, physical characteristics, habits or other behavioral characteristics, and fingerprints. For example, an alias sheet for Sam Nunnely recorded this information:

> Alias, Two-tone Sam; occupation, pop singer; D.O.B., May 20, 1988; height, 4' 2"; build, slim; hair, two-tone blonde and red, lots of curls; eyes, wide and blue; habits, leaves a trail of cookie crumbs and used Kleenex tissues, known to be allergic to dust and dogs, always seen wearing two-tone blue jeans.

Connect

Create a wall or bulletin board display using the thumbprint drawings and the alias sheets. Number each thumbprint drawing and mount these in a vertical or horizontal row. Mix up the alias sheets and mount them opposite the drawings (see figure 11.1). Have students carefully examine the swirls and lines of the thumbprints and match the drawings to the correct alias sheets.

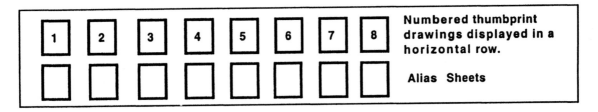

➤Figure 11.1. Alias/Thumbprint Drawing Display

➤Activity Plan 3: Can You Decipher It?

Engage

Ask students if they can decipher this message: SE CR ET COD ESA RE OLD ERT HAN JUL IUS CA ES AR This is a space cipher: The spaces between words are all that are changed. It reads "Secret codes are older than Julius Caesar." Have the students try this encoded message: NET TA RENROC EHT TA SU TEEM. This is a backward code: The message is written backwards. It reads "Meet us at the corner at ten." Explain to students that codes are used around the world in many contexts: Governments use them, military organizations use them, even young people use them; whenever someone wants to keep a message secret, a code is devised. (*Logical/Mathematical Intelligence*)

Elaborate

Have students work with the cipher code to gain experience in encoding and deciphering messages in preparation for creating their own secret codes. To construct the cipher code, have students write the letters of the alphabet in order across the page. They should then write a second row of letters directly below the first, but begin with the letter "D." D becomes A, E becomes B, F becomes C, etc. (see figure 11.2). Have students encode and exchange messages, then use the cipher code to decipher the messages. (*Logical/Mathematical Intelligence*)

A B C D E FG H I J K LMN O P Q R ST U VWX Y Z
W X Y A B C D E FGH IJ KL MNOPQRSTUVW Code

➤Figure 11.2. Cipher Code

Explore

Have students work in partnerships to create secret codes, then write messages using the secret code. Have them also give clues for deciphering the messages. (*Logical/Mathematical and Interpersonal Intelligences*)

Connect

Display the encoded messages and let students browse and try to decipher the messages.

➤ Activity Plan 4: Mystery Road Maps—Introduction

Materials

Mysteries for independent reading (one per student plus one to read aloud and use as a model)

Drawing paper

Illustrating materials (pencils, markers, crayons)

Tape (clear, wide)

Engage

Return to *Tuesday* to the double-page illustration where the detective is puzzling over the lily pads left in the street and the reporter is interviewing the man in the pajamas. Ask students how this page illustrates the ingredients for a mystery. (crime that hasn't been solved or a puzzling event that has not been explained, clues, witnesses, and a detective) (*Visual/Spatial Intelligence*)

In preparation for selecting mysteries for independent reading, briefly discuss the mysteries students have read or mystery writers they enjoy: What mysteries would you recommend? What mystery writers do you suggest we read?

Elaborate

Have students select mystery stories for independent reading, then share in a large circle (gather everyone into a large circle on the floor) about their selections. Based on cover illustrations, titles, and jacket information, speculate about the mystery events in their stories and make predictions about the development of the stories. As students share their ideas, record the titles of their books and highlights of their predictions.

Explore

Assign the first chapters of the books and pose these questions for reading: How did the beginnings of the stories match/differ from your predictions? What is the setting, who are the main characters, and what is the crime or unexplained mystery? (*Verbal/Linguistic Intelligence*)

Connect

Introduce the mystery road maps and explain the beginning assignments. Road map assignments assess the comprehension and literary analysis skills of the students and use pictures, road signs, and students' own words to trace a journey through the events of the stories and students' responses and interpretations (see figure 11.3). Sometimes road maps travel smoothly and in a straight line, but sometimes they twist and turn with the ups and downs of the plots. Road map assignments are completed as students predict, read, and respond to the chapters in their mysteries. (*Visual/Spatial and Verbal/Linguistic Intelligences*)

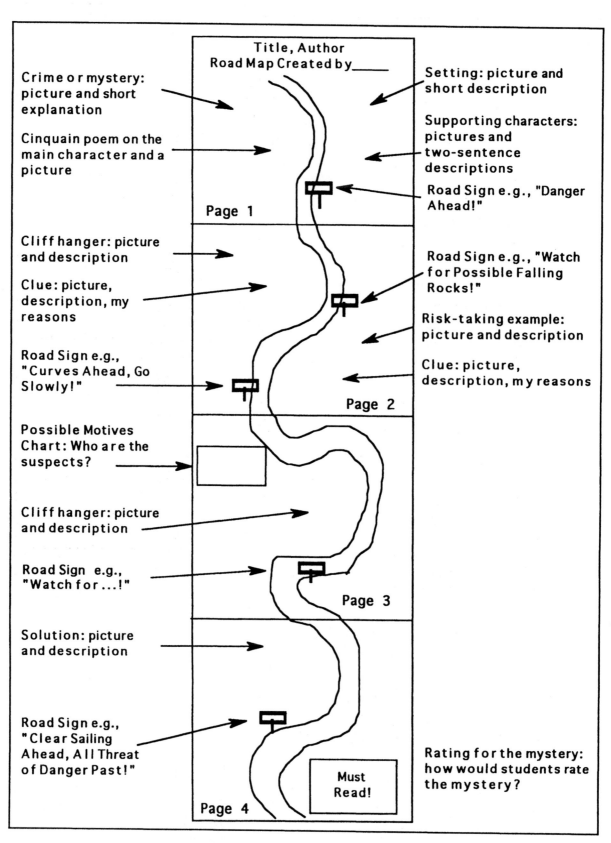

Crime or mystery: picture and short explanation

Cinquain poem on the main character and a picture

Setting: picture and short description

Supporting characters: pictures and two-sentence descriptions

Road Sign e.g., "Danger Ahead!"

Page 1

Cliff hanger: picture and description

Clue: picture, description, my reasons

Road Sign e.g., "Watch for Possible Falling Rocks!"

Risk-taking example: picture and description

Road Sign e.g., "Curves Ahead, Go Slowly!"

Clue: picture, description, my reasons

Page 2

Possible Motives Chart: Who are the suspects?

Cliff hanger: picture and description

Road Sign e.g., "Watch for...!"

Page 3

Solution: picture and description

Road Sign e.g., "Clear Sailing Ahead, All Threat of Danger Past!"

Must Read!

Rating for the mystery: how would students rate the mystery?

Page 4

➤ Figure 11.3. Mystery Road Maps

Starting the Road Map

1. Title and author of the mystery story.

2. Road map created by _____.

3. Draw and color the road for this first page of the map. (Depending on the lengths of the stories students have selected, the roads will continue through several sheets of paper. When students start fresh sheets of paper they should line up the previous pages with the new pages and have the roads continue without interruption.)

4. Draw a picture showing the setting of the story; write a short description of the setting telling place and time.

5. Describe the crime or mystery; add an illustration.

6. Write a cinquain poem introducing the main character of the story; add a picture of the main character. Cinquain poems should follow this pattern:

   • Line one: Name of the character.

   • Line two: State two adjectives about the main character.

   • Line three: List three verbs that tell actions of the main character (from the first chapter).

   • Line four: Write a four- to five-word phrase about an event of the first chapter that concerns the main character.

   • Line five: Write a one- to two-word synonym for the main character.

   Following is an example cinquain poem based on *Cam Jansen and the Chocolate Fudge Mystery* by David A. Adler, illustrated by Susanna Natti (New York: Viking, 1993).

   > *Jennifer Jansen*
   >
   > Red-haired, curious
   > walking door-to-door, selling, observing
   > "click," uses her photographic memory
   > "The Camera"

7. Describe and draw two supporting characters.

8. Draw a road sign that describes the atmosphere introduced by the events of the first chapter.

➤Activity Plan 5: Mystery Road Maps—Suspense

Materials

Tuesday by David Wiesner
Road maps from Activity Plan 4
Mysteries students are reading independently
Illustrating materials (markers, crayons, pencils)

Engage

Return to *Tuesday* to the illustration of the frogs approaching the neighborhood (seventh page after the title page) and discuss the suspense created by this illustration. Ask the students how the illustrator creates an atmosphere of suspense. (night, houses in darkness, feeling of expectation and potential trouble, wonder about the purpose of the frogs and what they will do) (*Visual/Spatial Intelligence*)

Elaborate

Gather students in large circle again, then write these words on the board or chart paper: *suspense, cliff-hanger, clue.* Continue the discussion on how they are used in mysteries. Ask students how they would define suspense. (uncertainty, apprehension, on the edge of your seat, an atmosphere of tension) As they review the events so far in their stories, how do students think suspense is created? Encourage them to use words from the authors in their responses.

Share an example of a cliff-hanger (a way of ending a chapter where the reader is left hanging about what will happen next). In the Cam Jansen story at the end of chapter two, Eric cautions Cam not to dig in the garbage because it might hold a bomb! The reader is left wondering if Cam will continue to open the trash can, if a bomb will really explode, or if it's all in Eric's imagination. Effective cliff-hangers create a great deal of suspense and make readers want to continue reading immediately just to find out what happens next. Have students turn to the last pages of their first chapters, determine if there are cliff-hangers, and share some examples.

Have students identify and discuss any clues they have learned that might help solve the mystery. Clues can be obvious ones like footprints in the snow, hairs on the carpet, or suspicious characters in dark glasses, but they can also be more obscure, like an unfinished crossword puzzle in a newspaper, the contents of a wastebasket, or a broken fingernail. Cam and Eric have discovered several possible clues: the woman in the raincoat and dark glasses, the bag of garbage placed in a neighbor's trash can rather than her own, and the old newspapers left at the yellow house. (*Verbal/Linguistic Intelligence*)

Explore

Have students read the next chapters in their stories and watch for words that would indicate suspense, clues, and cliff-hangers.

Connect

Have students continue building the road maps by adding the following assignments (*Visual/Spatial and Verbal/Linguistic Intelligences*):

1. Illustrate a "cliff-hanger" from chapter 1 or 2; write a description to accompany the picture.

2. Illustrate a "clue" from the second chapter; write a description to accompany the clue and explain why you think this is a clue.

3. Draw a road sign that shows "suspense" in the story.

➤Activity Plan 6: Mystery Road Maps—Taking a Risk

Materials

Road maps
Mysteries
Illustrating materials (markers, crayons, pencils)

Engage

Write this question on the board: "Taking a risk—is it worth it?" Then create a two-column chart labeled, "Yes, because" and "No, because." Have students give examples to discuss the concept of risk taking (see figure 11.4). (*Logical/Mathematical and Verbal/Linguistic Intelligences*)

Elaborate

Mystery writers often use risk to add suspense and excitement to their stories. Cam Jansen takes risks in her investigation of the chocolate fudge mystery. In chapters 4 and 5, she is determined to find out if someone is hiding in the yellow house and takes risks in exploring this suspicion, first by walking to the back of the yellow house to follow the woman in the dark glasses, then by hiding near the hedge so she has a clear view of the back door of the yellow house. Ask students to find and share examples of risk taking in the mystery stories they are reading.

Explore

Have students continue reading in their mystery stories and look for examples of risk taking.

Taking a Risk ... is it worth it?	
Yes, because ...	No, because ...
Yes, because you might discover a whole new land, like Christopher Columbus.	No, because mountain climbing without the right training and equipment is dangerous.
Yes, because you might discover the answer to the mystery.	No, because it's against the law and the wrong thing to do.
Yes, because standing up for the right stuff makes you feel good about yourself.	

➤Figure 11.4. Risk Taking Chart

Connect

Have students continue creating the road maps by adding the following assignments (*Visual/Spatial and Verbal/Linguistic Intelligences*):

1. Illustrate an example of "risk taking" from the chapters you have read; write a description to accompany the picture.

2. Illustrate another "clue"; write a description to accompany the clue and explain why you think this is a clue.

3. Draw a road sign that shows the continuing "suspense" of the story.

➤ Activity Plan 7: Mystery Road Maps— Looking at Motives

Materials

Road maps
Mysteries
Illustrating materials (markers, crayons, pencils)

Engage

Create a three-column "possible motives" chart on the board and have students choose suspects from their stories to help complete the chart (see figure 11.5). List the characters from the stories in the left column, describe behaviors that make the characters suspicious in the middle column, and speculate about the possible motives of the characters in the right column.

Looking at Motives		
Characters	**Suspicious Behaviors**	**Possible Motives**
The man	He arrives in the middle of the night, he doesn't speak, he carries Mama's locket in his pouch, he wants Molly and Nathan to follow him.	He's the one who caused Pa's disappearance and doesn't want anyone to find Molly and Nathan; **or**, someone else made Pa disappear and the man wants to help and brought the locket so Molly and Nathan would come with him.
Mrs. Becker	She threatens the boy with an ax when they try to visit her.	She knows more about Grandpa's death and Snake Dancer's Cave and the gold than she should; **or**, other people have been bothering her property and she's worried something else will be stolen.

➤ Figure 11.5. What Is the Motive?

Elaborate

Mystery writers usually include information about motives in their stories. Sometimes the information is revealed through the conversations of the main characters and sometimes the suspects unveil this information. If readers carefully analyze the motive information, it is often possible to solve the mystery.

Have students return to the possible motives chart and analyze the motives. Ask them to identify what other motives the characters might have for the same action. For example, Cam Jansen thinks the woman in dark glasses threw away the garbage in the neighbor's can because she has evidence from a crime that she wants to hide. Eric offers an alternative and suggests that she had a late-night party and has more garbage than will fit in her can. She's wearing dark glasses because her eyes hurt and a raincoat because she's still in her pajamas.

Explore

Have students continue to read in their mystery stories, then take stock of the situations in their books by answering these questions: Who are the suspects, what behaviors make them suspects, and what are their motives?

Connect

Add the following assignments to the road maps (*Visual/Spatial and Verbal/Linguistic Intelligences*):

1. Create your own possible motives charts and add these to your road maps. Begin with the characters you shared with the class and add at least one other suspicious character to the charts. List the characters in the left column, describe the suspicious behaviors in the middle column, and explain possible motives in the right column, just as in the modeled example (see figure 11.5).

2. Illustrate another cliff-hanger from the story and write a description to accompany the picture.

3. Analyze the motives chart and create a road sign that points a finger at the person responsible for the mystery.

➤ Activity Plan 8: Mystery Road Maps—Solutions

Materials

Road maps
Mysteries
Illustrating materials (markers, crayons, pencils)
Clear tape

Engage

Write these words on the board and dramatically recite them: "Way to go! You figured it out again!" Gather in a large circle and discuss possible solutions with the students. Ask them: If you were the authors of the stories, what would be your solutions to the mysteries you have been reading?

Elaborate

Have students finish reading their mysteries, then meet with small groups of students to compare their solutions with their predictions.

Explore

Have students finish the road maps by adding the following assignments (*Visual/Spatial and Verbal/Linguistic Intelligences*):

1. Illustrate and explain the solution to the mystery.

2. Create a final road sign for the story.

Connect

Use the clear tape to connect the road map pages and create a display of the road maps. Gather students in a final large circle discussion and ask them to share evaluations of the mysteries they read, responding to these questions: Would you recommend your mysteries to other students? Why or why not?

➤ Activity Plan 9: Creating a Mystery Magazine

Note: The mystery magazine project is an opportunity for students to work in a real-world simulation as they join editorial teams and take on editorial and writing responsibilities.

Materials

Gavel
Selection of children's magazines (*Ranger Rick, Cobblestone,* etc.)
Transparency of the magazine job roles and responsibilities (see figure 11.6)

Editor In Chief (Teacher performs this role.)	Leads meetings of the class and makes final decisions.
Editor/Contributor	•Leads and encourages the team. •Makes assignments. •Brings questions to the Editor in Chief. •Prepares a magazine article. •Meets with other editors.
Layout Editor/ Contributor	•Designs the masthead for the section. •Prepares a "mock-up" of the page. •Leads meeting to discuss and revise the mock-up; accepts suggestions and ideas about the arrangement of the page. •Prepares a magazine article. •Meets with other layout editors.
Headline Editor/ Contributor	•Writes all headlines for the page. •Uses the computer to create all the headlines for the page. •Contributes a magazine article. •Meets with other headline editors.
Proofreader/ Contributor	•Edits the magazine section for spelling, capitalization, and punctuation errors. •Contributes a magazine article. •Meets with other proofreaders.
Circulation Director/ Contributor	•Meets with other circulation directors to plan how to share the magazine. •Contributes a magazine article.

➤Figure 11.6. Magazine Job Roles

Engage

Simulate an editorial meeting (you are the editor in chief), introduce the mystery magazine, and have students browse the selected magazines to gather ideas for types of assignments.

To begin the meeting, tap the gavel and call the meeting to order: "Welcome to the mystery writers' magazine editorial meeting. It's exciting to see so many interested writers and I'm eager to see the magazine we will produce. When you think about creating a mystery magazine, what ideas come to mind?" (Students will probably share that the magazine should include lots of mystery puzzle ideas and some mystery stories.) Continue the meeting: "We have a few ideas for the mystery magazine; let's take a moment and look at some magazines to see what we might add. What kinds of stories and information do you find in these magazines? How might they work in the mystery magazine?" (Have students browse the magazines to find what might be added to the mystery magazine. Some responses might be that in addition to the puzzles and mystery stories, the magazine might also have reviews, interviews, current events information, letters, feature stories, cartoons, and/or mystery pictures.) (*Verbal/Linguistic Intelligence*)

Elaborate

There are other elements besides the articles that go into making a magazine. Have students look at the covers of the magazines: Covers give the names of the magazines and the months and years of publication. Ask students how the editors make readers want to pick up the magazines and read them. (Responses may be interesting titles, attention-getting pictures or writing, use of color and/or bold, enlarged print, and/or placement of the art.)

Address the students as follows:

> As you look again at the contents of the magazines, what do you notice about the structure of the magazines' contents? [number of columns, placement of the table of contents, colors, fonts, sizes of titles, uses of pictures to accompany text, and/or length of articles] These decisions are all made by the editors of the magazines. Let's look at some of the jobs that help create a magazine, because these will be the roles we take on to create the mystery magazine. As you listen to the jobs and their responsibilities and skills, think about your interests and skills and which job you could most capably perform.

Explore

Review magazine job descriptions and describe the responsibilities and skills for each position. See figure 11.6 for a summary of the job responsibilities and use the following descriptive information to explain each job:

> Editors will be the leaders for the teams. In addition to writing articles for the magazine and meeting with the other editors to design and create the cover of the magazine, editors will lead team meetings, help team members select assignments, and encourage team members to stay on task and

complete their assignments. If team members have questions that you can-not answer, it will be your responsibility to bring those questions to the editor in chief. Think about this role if you work well with other students and take leadership positions easily and effectively.

Layout editors decide the arrangement of the contents of the magazine. You look at the contributions from your team members and design and share a "mock-up" or first draft showing how you would arrange the art, the titles, and the text of these contributions. After discussing the layout drafts with team members, you make any necessary revisions and prepare the final copies. You also contribute articles and design the section head-ings (mastheads) for the magazine. [See figure 11.7 for an example of a masthead.] Think about this role if you have artistic and design skills.

➤ Figure 11.7. Sample Masthead Design

Headline editors read the articles contributed by team members and write the titles or headlines that accompany the articles; for example, an article about the Bermuda Triangle was entitled "Here Comes Trouble!"; an article about Amelia Earhart began with "Where Is She?"; a secret code puzzle had the headline "Ready, Aim, Solve!"; and an original mystery story was introduced with "The Good Luck Story." Once titles are written, headline editors use computers to design the titles (color, size, style, and font). They also write articles for the magazine. Think about this job if you are creative with words and enjoy designing on a computer.

Proofreaders write articles for the magazine and make final editing correc-tions (spelling, capitalization, and punctuation) on the contributions from team members. Think about this role if you are an accomplished speller and knowledgeable about punctuation.

Circulation directors will decide how to share the magazine with others in the school and will make presentations to build excitement and interest in reading the magazine. Think about this role if you are comfortable speaking before groups and have a flair for the dramatic.

Connect

Have students list first and second choice preferences for the jobs they want and write a sentence or two describing their qualifications for their choices. Review preference statements and divide students into teams (for example, a reviews team, an interviews team, a puzzles team, a current events team, a features team, and/or an original mystery stories team) and designate roles. Each team can have an editor, a layout editor, a headline editor, a proofreader, and a circulation director, but adjust as necessary according to the size of the class. The proofreader and headline editor jobs could be combined and the editor and circulation director jobs could be completed by one student. (*Interpersonal Intelligence*)

➤Activity Plan 10: Mystery Magazine Assignments

Materials

large index cards (one per student)
K-W-L Chart (activity sheet 11.2, one per student)

Engage

Write these words on the board: *Who? What? Where? When?* Start a mystery for your class. (Figure 11.8 illustrates this process.) Give a large index card to each student. In step one students should write responses to one of these questions: Who did it? or Who is the detective? Encourage students to be elaborate in their descriptions; instead of just naming a character, they should describe the character (e.g., a red-haired detective with a love for chocolate). Have students pass the index cards to the right. The next students must use what is written on the cards to write responses to a "what" question, such as What happened? They then pass again to the right and the next students answer a "where" question, such as Where did it happen? The last students to get the cards answer a "when" question, such as When did it happen? Share the results.

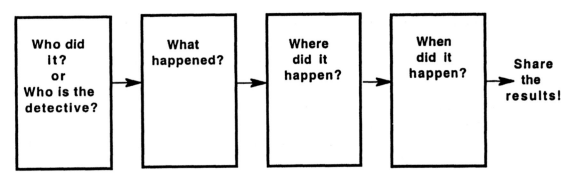

➤Figure 11.8. Start Your Own Mystery

K-W-L Chart

Topic:

Know What I know about the topic	Want What I want to know	Learned What I learned from my research

▶ Activity Sheet 11.2. K-W-L Chart

Elaborate

Hold a second editorial meeting: Announce teams and roles, list magazine section choices, and have editors lead team meetings to discuss and select sections.

To begin the second meeting, tap the gavel and call the meeting to order: "Welcome to our second editorial meeting. After carefully reviewing your preference statements and thinking about the needs of the magazine, the editor in chief has made these team and role decisions. Remember that the decisions about the teams were made because you each have important contributions to make and the editor in chief felt your skills were needed in the roles you were assigned." (Announce the teams and the roles.)

"Here are the magazine sections we brainstormed at our first meeting." (List the sections students brainstormed: puzzles, original mystery stories, reviews, interviews, current events information, letters, feature stories, cartoons, etc.) "Editors will perform their first responsibilities and lead team discussions to select the section of the magazine that will be your team's assignment. If more than one team wants a section, we will take a vote and the team closest to guessing the identified number will have that section."

Once magazine sections have been chosen, return to the whole class editorial meeting format and brainstorm magazine assignment ideas (see figure 11.9 for possible ideas). Categorize the assignment ideas into the appropriate magazine sections and have editors continue team meetings to make assignments for each team member.

Explore

Have the students use the K-W-L strategy (see activity sheet 11.2) to begin preliminary planning. Students should use the first column to write facts they already know about their topics, the second column to write questions for research, and the third column to record the results of their research.

Have students conduct research, prepare rough drafts (integrating their research notes), and conference with peers and the editor in chief to revise their rough drafts. Once rough drafts are revised, students should follow this step-by-step process:

1. Consult with the proofreader to edit the rough draft (spelling, punctuation, capitalization).

2. Share the magazine article with the headline editor to let the headline editor compose a headline.

3. Produce a final revised and edited copy.

4. Plan and create a graphic for the article.

5. Take final copy and graphic to the layout editor. (Figure 11.10 shows the entire process at a glance.)

Reviews	mystery books and authors, mystery movies, television mystery programs
Interviews	detectives, police, FBI agents
Puzzles	board games, secret codes, fingerprints, word finds
Current Events	things happening in the news that are puzzling or mysterious (Note: this is a challenging section and should be assigned to students who enjoy more difficult assignments.)
Mystery Stories	original stories written by the students
Feature Stories	famous detectives in history and in literature, mysterious topics, e.g., •**pyramids**, •**Stonehenge**, •**Easter Island**: Who built the interesting statues found on the island? •**Rosetta Stone**: Why were the hieroglyphics a puzzle for so many years? •**ancient astronauts**: Why do scientists thinks the lines of Nazca are the work of ancient astronauts? •**black holes** •**mermaids** •**Atlantis** •**Amelia Earhart** •**unidentified flying objects**: How do scientists explain UFO's? •**Bigfoot** •**Bermuda Triangle**, •**northern lights**: How are they formed and why do they happen? •**Hope Diamond**: What is the mystery surrounding the diamond? •**Loch Ness monster**: Does the monster exist?

➤Figure 11.9. Mystery Magazine Assignment Ideas

Magazine Assignments

Beginning the Assignment:

1. Use the K-W-L chart to begin planning the research:

   K: Write what you already know about the topic.

   W: Write your questions for research.

2. Conduct research and record your notes in the "L" column of your chart.

3. Use your research notes to prepare a rough draft.

4. Conference with peers and the editor in chief to revise your rough drafts.

Finishing the Assignment:

1. Consult with a proofreader to edit the rough draft (spelling, punctuation, capitalization).

2. Share the magazine article with the headline editor to let the headline editor compose a headline.

3. Produce a final revised and edited copy.

4. Plan and create a graphic for the article.

5. Take final copy and graphic to the layout editor.

➤ Figure 11.10. Magazine Assignment Procedure

While students are pursuing individual assignments, hold editorial meetings with editors, proofreaders, and circulation directors:

Editors' meeting: Help editors brainstorm ideas to name the magazine and design the cover.

Layout editors' meeting: Discuss and make design decisions about the headings for the sections. (See figure 11.7 for a masthead example.) Design the headings.

Headline editors' meeting: Review newspaper headlines and practice headline writing and creating headlines using a computer.

Proofreaders' meeting: Practice editing a sample magazine article.

Circulation directors' meeting: Plan magazine distribution.

Connect

Publish and distribute the magazine. If copying facilities are available, have multiple copies made.

12 *Introducing the Caldecott Award: Randolph Caldecott*

➤ Activity Plan: A Look at Randolph Caldecott

Materials

Selection of Caldecott Award books that show the gold medal

Audiovisual resource on Randolph Caldecott (*Randolph Caldecott: The Man Behind the Medal* is one suggestion. It's a video from Weston Woods, 12 Oakwood Ave., Norwalk, CT 06850, 800-243-5020; cost: $39.00.)

Picture books illustrated by Randolph Caldecott

Various resources giving information about Randolph Caldecott (Most encyclopedias have information, and you can use the Internet to access the Randolph Caldecott home page at http://www.ala.org/alsc/caldecott.html.)

Preplanning with the librarian (In addition to the book chosen as the Caldecott Award winner each year, honor books are also named. Gather a selection of honor books so that each student in the class will have one for independent reading; a list of honor books is available through this Internet site: http://www.ala.org/alsc/caldecott.html.)

Chart paper

Drawing paper

Illustrating materials (crayons, colored pencils, markers)

Transparency of figure 12.1

Engage

Display the Caldecott Award books and point to the gold medals. Ask students what criteria they would use to determine gold medal books. (Create a web listing their answers; see figure 12.2 for some anticipated responses.)

The Caldecott Award program began in 1938, and it was named in honor of Randolph Caldecott, a nineteenth-century illustrator of children's books and stories.

Cinquain Poem Form

Name
Two describing words (adjectives)
Three action words (verbs)
Four-word phrase giving new information about the person
One- or two-word synonym for the person

Eric Carle
Bold, brilliant
Imagined, wrote, illustrated
A Very Hungry Caterpillar
Author

Stair Poem Form

One- or two-word synonym for the person

Four-word phrase telling the location of the person

Three describing words

Name of the person

Great inventor
Experimenting in his laboratory
Imaginative, creative genius
Thomas Edison

➤ Figure 12.1. Rules for Writing Cinquain and Stair Poems

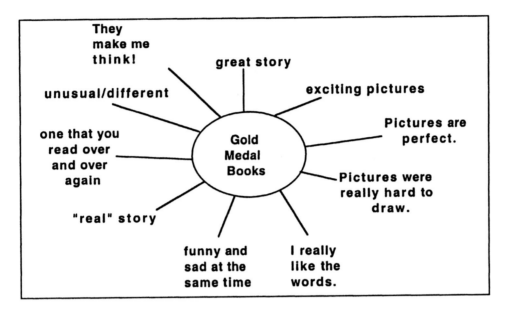

➤ Figure 12.2. Criteria for Choosing Gold Medal Books

Elaborate

Show the class the Caldecott program. Set a purpose for viewing: As you watch and listen, why do you think the library association named the award in honor of Randolph Caldecott? Refocus question: How was his style of illustrating "gold medal" quality? (Lifelike characters and scenes filled with humor, imagination, and action seem to be characteristics of his illustrations.)

Have students work with partners to gather more information about Caldecott. (In preparation for this research, bookmark the Internet site cited in the materials list; encourage some partnerships to begin with the encyclopedias while other partnerships use the Internet site. Circulate and flip-flop sources when you see students may need second sources.)

Explore

Use figure 12.1 to model and give directions on writing cinquain or stair poems. Have students use their research information to write cinquain or stair poems about the life and work of Randolph Caldecott. Post a portrait of Caldecott (available from the Web site listed above) in the center of the bulletin board; have students present their poems to the class. Then display the poems around the portrait. (*Verbal/Linguistic and Interpersonal Intelligences*)

Connect

Travel to the library to select Caldecott Honor books for independent reading. After students read the books, have them draw pictures of favorite scenes from the books and label the pictures with titles and authors. Before adding the pictures to the bulletin board display, have students present their pictures to the class, give brief summaries of the stories, and explain why they think the books were chosen as award-winning or honor books. (*Verbal/Linguistic and Visual/Spatial Intelligences*)

Glossary

Acrylics: pigments that dry quickly; can be used thick or thinned with water

Casein: pigments made from milk curds

Charcoal: soft, burnt-wood sticks or pencils

Collage: materials and objects pasted over a surface

Colored pencils: colored graphite pencils

Gesso: white pigment mixed with whiting, water, and glue; used to size (prepare) the canvas

Glaze: layer of transparent color applied over the body color

Gouache: pigments mixed with white chalk and water that become opaque when applied

Graphite: soft carbon, used in pencils instead of lead

Gums: binding mediums

India ink: drawing ink made from gas black and adhesive

Inks: transparent dyes

Line drawings: pictures drawn using lines, usually not including tone or shading

Lithographic pencil: compound of grease, wax, and lampblack

Oil pastels: pigments mixed with chalk, oil, and gum and dried and formed into crayons

Oils: pigments used with turpentine or linseed oil; may be opaque or transparent

Pastel paper: textured paper

Pastels: pigments mixed with chalk, water, and gum and dried and formed into crayons

Pen and ink: drawings made using dip pens and a variety of inks

Pigments: powdered colors made from natural (rocks, earth, plants, fruit, insects, and shellfish) and chemical substances

Tempera: pigments emulsified with oil and egg

Wash: highly diluted and thinned application of color

Watercolors: very finely ground pigments that are combined with gum and mixed with water

Whiting: very finely ground powdered chalk

Woodcuts: designs cut into well-seasoned, dried wood

Index

About the Author

Shan Glandon works in the Jenks Public Schools as a library media specialist and teaches summer courses at Tulsa Community College. She is active in the Oklahoma Library Association and conducts workshops and presentations on implementing flexible scheduling and connecting the library to the classroom. In her spare time she loves to read, bike ride, and enjoy the arts (plays, concerts, museums, and art galleries).